THE Daredevil BOOK FOR Cats

THE Daredevil BOOK FOR Cats

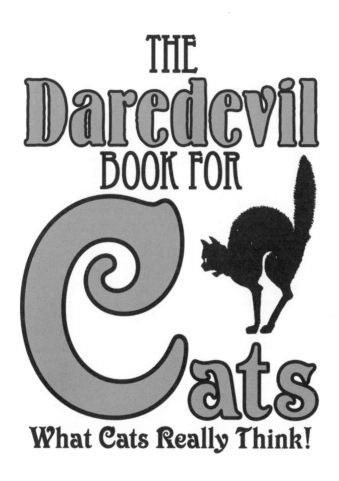

What Cats Really Think!

NICK GRIFFITHS

ILLUSTRATED BY DAVID MOSTYN

CHARTWELL
BOOKS, INC.

Nick Griffiths is an author and journalist because NASA wouldn't let him be an astronaut. He has written *Dalek I Loved You: A Memoir* and *Who Goes There*, both based around Doctor Who, and the comic novel *In the Footsteps of Harrison Dextrose*, while writing largely for *Radio Times*. He owns a cat named Columbo, who has failed to solve any murder cases, and would love to own a dog but can't get past the idea of picking up its poo in a small plastic bag.

Illustrator **David Mostyn** began his career as a commercial artist in advertising, then moved into publishing and set up his own company Mostyn Partners in 1977. David has worked for 30 years in comic strips, producing drawings for DC Thomson, Marvel Comics and DC Comics, among others. He is married with two children and one cat, and lives in Oxford.

This edition printed in 2009 by

CHARTWELL BOOKS, INC.

A Division of **BOOK SALES, INC.**

276 Fifth Avenue Suite 206
New York, New York 10001 USA

Copyright © 2009 Arcturus Publishing Limited/ Nick Griffiths

26/27 Bickels Yard, 151–153 Bermondsey Street, London SE1 3HA

ISBN-13: 978-0-7858-2576-0
ISBN-10: 0-7858-2576-2
AD000141EN

Printed in China

Contents

Introduction

Hello there. My name is Prince Cuddles. Yes, I know. It's a cross I have to bear, and the inevitable outcome when your family allows their youngest to name the new kitten. (The person who named me is called Tarquin, though I have always preferred simply That Little Git, even if he's quite big now.)

You can call me Al, as my friends do. It rolls off the tongue a bit more quickly – and there is no point in doing anything that takes longer than 'quickly', unless it is napping. I could nap forever, and sometimes do. After all, I'm getting on a bit now – 53 in cat years – though I consider myself to be in the prime of my life. Indeed, there are none more gorgeous, witty or self-confident. Let me tell you a little bit about myself.

There are five human servants – as I like to think of them – in my family. They are: mother and father, Sheila and Dick, two sons, the aforesaid git Tarquin and his little bro Rocco, as well as a daughter known as Stella. They all love me very much and I, in turn, don't mind them, sort of. They're not too bad, though I strongly suspect I deserve better.

I LIVE BY THE CAT DOCTRINE, WHICH STATES:

1. Just as the Earth revolves around the Sun, so the world revolves around us. That is how it should be.

2. If a job is worth doing, it's worth being done by someone else. (Our human servants, more often than not.)

3. We are great, and being great is exhausting work. Thus we should lounge around as often and for as long as possible. It's only reasonable.

4. If we wanted to be disturbed, we would hang 'DO DISTURB' notices on our noses. You will notice that we do not.

5. However, we are not arrogant creatures – well, only a little bit – so in payment for our human servants' efforts, we sometimes allow ourselves to be scratched, hugged, fed, watered and generally mollycoddled. That is why we are great.

6. Mice and small birds are NOT our friends.

You are holding a Very Important Book (VIB) in your paws. I have been asked to write it on account of my experience and modest greatness. Think of it as a design for cat life, a bible for the feline. You might think this overstates the case: I would have to disagree and you will too once you have read the words which tumble from my golden pen. Up until now, there has been a gaping chasm in the market place. I humbly believe this masterpiece fills it quite nicely, thank you.

Within these pages, you will discover (among many other gems):

Why humans are less clever than lettuce.

Why wearing a hat won't necessarily make you a good poet.

Why the moon will disappear in 2037.

How to avoid being neutered by strategically deploying two pickled walnuts and a cocktail sausage.

🐱 What Charles Dickens really meant when he said, 'What greater gift than the love of a cat?'

🐱 Why Dick Whittington was the weak link in the 'Dick Whittington and his cat' operation.

🐱 The proper etiquette when encountering another feline in limited space.

🐱 Plus all manner of indispensable historical and factual information.

Pay rapt attention to my words and you too could become almost as great as me. But first, since writing is pretty tiring, a short nap, I think…

Origin of the Species

Hard to believe, I know, but cats never underwent evolution. They didn't need to – we were born perfect to start with! Everything else evolved from us, that's if you can call it evolution. I mean, look what we ended up with. Pathetic really. Here's a handy chart to show you what I am getting at:

LENGTH OF TIME TO EVOLVE FROM CAT

Dinosaur: 1.2 million years   **Shark:** 2.5 million years

Human: 16 million years   **Lettuce:** 18 million years

Do you see now? (I realize this may be quite taxing for some readers.) So humans, dinosaurs, sharks and lettuces, for instance, have evolved – from cats, I stress again – over millions of years. The box above shows how long it took in each case.

Am I suggesting that the lettuce is superior to the human? Yes, I am.

So cats were the first beings to walk the Earth, and it would have been pretty boring had we not had each other for company. There were squabbles and disagreements, fights even, I would concur, but generally we had a fab time.

A TYPICAL CAT CONVERSATION BACK THEN WENT A BIT LIKE THIS:

CAT 1: Hello, how are you?

CAT 2: I am very well, thank you. How are you?

CAT 1: Very well! My, you're looking very handsome today!

CAT 2: Why thank you! If I may say so, you are looking exceedingly handsome today, too!

CAT 1: You may say so. Thank you.

CAT 2: I do feel my teeth might be a little shinier than yours.

CAT 1: Oh. Do you now?

CAT 2: Yes, I do.

CAT 1: Well, I'd suggest that my claws are far sharper than yours – and infinitely more carefully manicured.

Cat 2: Oh. Would you now? Well, your fur looks like some matted old grass I found in a swamp.

Cat 1: You think so, do you? Well your head looks like something I left in a toilet. Eight weeks ago.

[A snarling fight ensues, which ceases only when Cat 1 realizes that Cat 2 was his reflection in a mirror.]

Author's note: The important thing to remember is that we cats were there at the very dawn of civilization, providing an example for all the other creatures to live up to. The situation became pretty dicey once the dinosaurs arrived (and the sharks weren't a great deal friendlier), but all it took was a little bit of patience – a wait of 16 million years – until the arrival of the humans. And then we could wind them around our little claws. Still do. Still do.

How Did Cats Become Domesticated?

The fact that cats don't actually need humans doesn't mean that it isn't often nice and convenient to share premises. You scratch my back and I'll scratch yours (if I'm feeling specially energetic). Let me put it to you this way…
We used to live here:

Then humans came along and invited us to live here:

Which would you choose? It ain't brain surgery.

A Week in the Life...

Humans seem to think of cats as languid creatures, forever sleeping. They'd be amazed at what is really going on in our peerless minds. To dispel any false notions, here's an average week from my diary...

Monday
Got up, washed, cleaned teeth.
Had a wee.
Invented new type of plastic.
Received Nobel Prize for Economics.
Went to bed.

Tuesday
Got up, washed, cleaned teeth.
Had a wee.
Test-piloted new Mars probe.
Suggested some crucial tinkering.
Graduated from Harvard.
Went to bed.

Wednesday
Got up, washed, cleaned teeth.
Had a wee.
Introduced to the Queen.
I asked her what she did.
Cured world poverty.
Went to bed.

Thursday
Got up, washed, cleaned teeth.
Had a wee.
Completed New York Marathon.
Ran it again, since was not out of breath.
Up all night boozing with Sarah Palin.

Friday
Got up, washed, cleaned teeth.
Had a wee.
Hangover.
Slept till Monday. (Hey – I deserved it!)

The Ten Commandments of Cats

1. Feel free to covet your neighbouring cat's wife. And their house. And their Kitty Chunks, for that matter.

2. It's OK to kill, provided the creature you're killing is smaller than you and defenceless. No sense taking risks.

3. If a human offers you left-over kebab - leave it. Honestly, I always have terrible trouble the next morning.

4. Never explain. We're meant to be mysterious.

5. Learn your spellings. Idol ⇒ bad. Idle ⇒ good.

6. Commit adultery. If anyone challenges your morals, tell them there aren't enough cats to go around according to a recent survey. (If they ask which survey, run away.)

7. Never repay a favour. Giving should be its own reward.

8. If a job's worth doing, it's worth getting someone else to do it.

9. Always get into fights. No idea why.

10. There is only one god. That's you, my good friend.

How To... Wheedle Around
Your Human Servants

After getting the hang of doing naff all most of the time, this is the Second Most Important Thing You Will Ever Learn. It requires a careful balancing act, between obsequiousness ('Will you do that for me, pretty please?') and outrage ('You'd blooming well better do that for me, you lazy git!').

To become a master of this act of wheedling requires an intense knowledge of human psychology. What makes them tick? What pulls their strings? If I paw them now, will it be irritating or endearing? To ensure my expertise in this arena, I have read a vast number of psychology books. (Well, when I said 'read', I meant 'brushed past'. Actually, when I said 'brushed past' I meant 'been in the same building as'. Or rather, when I said 'I have been in the same building as a vast number of psychology books' what I actually meant was 'I lay around for ages and if all the psychology books in the world had been burned to cinders, I would not have given a monkey's.' So I think we can safely call me an Expert in the Field.)

So this is how to wheedle around your human servants. Work your way down the list until one of these ploys strikes gold:

1. Lie around doing naff all, hoping that by some miracle of ESP they realize what you're after and produce it. (This rarely works, which doesn't stop me from trying it.)

2. Look at them with your cutest expression.

3. Add purring to 2 (above).

If necessary, take their goldfish hostage.

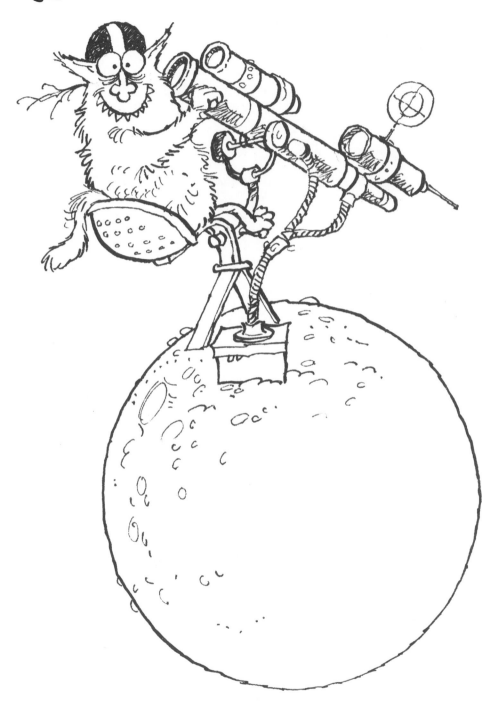

4. Paw at them, making insistent 'miaow' sounds.

5. Rub yourself around their ankles. (I find this degrading.)

6. Start moaning. Something like this: 'Riaow riaow mrrw riaow RAOW RAOW!'

7. Bite their ankles.

8. Take their goldfish hostage.

9. Eat the goldfish.

10. Take their children hostage.

11. Let the children go (you were only bluffing), but set fire to the kitchen.

12. While the kitchen burns, call in a nuclear air strike.

13. Unlucky for some! Having destroyed their entire town/city – this is starting to feel a tad personal, I will grant you – become the head of a James Bond-style world domination organization, buy a very big laser, plant it on the moon and hold all of Planet Earth to ransom.

I reckon that should do it. If they haven't topped up your water dish by now, I'd recommend changing families.

The Rules of Engagement

What do you do when you come across another cat in a narrow space? Do you smile, tip your hat and step aside to let him saunter by? Or do you have a bit more about you? What exactly are the Rules of Engagement?

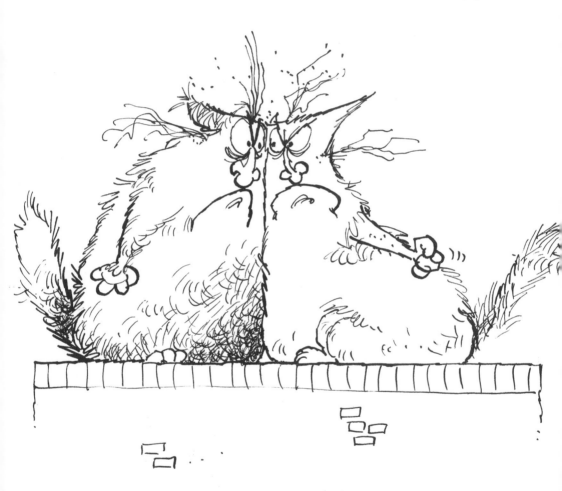

1. Think to yourself, 'Might this other cat actually be friendly?'

2. Think to yourself, 'It's quite feasible that we might get on!'

3. Think to yourself, 'We could even become best mates in time!'

4. Think to yourself, 'Who knows, in a couple of weeks we might be hanging out together, swapping tales of derring-do and sharing a discarded kipper? Why be hasty?'

5. Launch yourself at this upstart and attempt to scratch his butt-ugly eyes out.

We're cats. We can't help it.

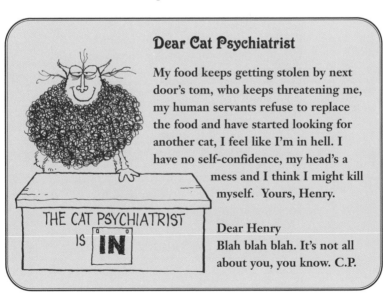

Dear Cat Psychiatrist

My food keeps getting stolen by next door's tom, who keeps threatening me, my human servants refuse to replace the food and have started looking for another cat, I feel like I'm in hell. I have no self-confidence, my head's a mess and I think I might kill myself. Yours, Henry.

Dear Henry
Blah blah blah. It's not all about you, you know. C.P.

THE CAT PSYCHIATRIST IS **IN**

How To... Catch a Mouse

It's in our DNA, of course. We hate meeces to pieces and we hunt them down with the dexterity, guile and skill of the cheetah (while being smaller, less rustic and less spotty). However, should your DNA be failing you, or if you are simply rusty, here are some useful tips on mouse-catching...

ALWAYS TREAT YOUR PREY WITH RESPECT

Only kidding! When you catch your mouse, toy with it for ages. In my younger days, I was known to tape a caught mouse to the side of a Monopoly board and force it to play the game with me, before finally despatching it. (I used to tell the sucker that I'd let it go if it let me win. Heheh.)

STAY DOWNWIND

Obviously there isn't much wind in a house – however, there may be air-conditioning to consider, or one of your human servants (probably the eldest male) may fart a lot. Make sure you're behind any such air propagators.

ALWAYS CARRY CHEESE

Mice love cheese, that's a fact, and nothing to do with the stuff in cartoons. I always carry a lump of Cheddar in my back pocket, just in case. Simply place it on the floor and wait. Those meeces won't be able to resist! Then: pounce!

Incidentally, did you know? The moon is made of cheese, and mice sent up by the Americans on Apollos 16 and 17 are frantically nibbling away at its surface. Experts estimate that they will have eaten the moon all up by 2037, when it will disappear from our night sky forever. (Another good reason to hate meeces.)

WEAR CAMOUFLAGE

Easy enough in wooded areas. Less easy in a house. Whenever my human servants are decorating, or laying new floor coverings, I demand that they save me a section of their materials, be it some wallpaper or carpeting. Then I can wrap that around me and become completely invisible.

PUT YOUR PREY AT ITS EASE

If the mouse is uptight, it won't be easy to
catch. So I urge you to play some soothing
music – Mantovani, say – and lower the
lights. Some candles in the offing and
perhaps a bunch of red roses might also do
the trick. Let them know you care. (Before
you eat their head for dinner.)

Some Uses for a Dead Mouse

There's no sense just killing the thing. We are hunters and we do not kill for sport, which is a mere frippery; we kill because it is in our genes. And the first rule of hunting is: always shut the gate after you.

No, sorry, I'm getting confused with the Country Code. The first rule of hunting is: never waste your prey. Yes, that's more like it. So I've thought up some handy uses for a dead mouse (see opposite page):

1. STAGE YOUR OWN OLYMPIC FIELD EVENTS!

2. CONDUCT AN ORCHESTRA!

3. AS A...

Hoi, you, what do you think you're doing?

You're not supposed to eat it! Oh, just forget it then.

Cat Quotes (And What They Really Mean)

'**What greater gift than the love of a cat?**' – CHARLES DICKENS
I'm terribly sorry, I appear to be all out of presents.

'**One cat just leads to another.**' – ERNEST HEMINGWAY
Never ask a cat for directions.

'**Never wear anything that panics the cat.**'– PJ O'ROURKE
Golfers should steer clear of cats.

'**Time spent with cats is never wasted.**' – ANON
I know I lost my job, Mom – but I still have Mr Tiddles. Ow,
Mom, stop hitting me with the broom!

'You see, wire telegraph is a kind of a very, very long cat. You pull his tail in New York and his head is meowing in Los Angeles. Do you understand this? And radio operates exactly the same way: you send signals here, they receive them there. The only difference is that there is no cat.' –
ALBERT EINSTEIN (ASKED TO DESCRIBE HOW A RADIO WORKS)
I must admit, I'm a little baffled myself.

'The smallest feline is a masterpiece.' – LEONARDO DA VINCI
The Mona Lisa's over-rated.

'I like pigs. Dogs look up to us. Cats look down on us. Pigs treat us as equals.' – WINSTON CHURCHILL
Two bacon sandwiches, please.

'We should be careful to get out of an experience only the wisdom that is in it, and stop there; lest we be like the cat that sits down on a hot stove-lid. She will never sit down on a hot stove-lid again, and that is well; but she will never sit down on a cold one anymore, either.'
– MARK TWAIN
You'll never learn anything if you cook with gas.

'Thousands of years ago, cats were worshipped as gods. Cats have never forgotten this.' – ANON
And you thought elephants had long memories!

'Cats are intended to teach us that not everything in nature has a function.' – GARRISON KEILLOR
Cats are like men's nipples.

Fat Cats

Odd one, this. Human servants come up with so much utter drivel. They pretend the nonsense they spout is 'living language'. For example, here's a 100 per cent genuine 'fat cat', the real thing:

It's a cat, clearly. Yet humans have appropriated the phrase 'fat cat' to describe another human who hoards other people's money with no qualms, who is odious and overweight – but I just don't see the link between the two.

A human 'fat cat' looks something like this:

No, hang on, I think I get it now.

Cats Versus Dogs

No two creatures could be less alike. Where dogs have masters, we have staff. They fetch; we look fetching. They pant; we purrspire. If further proof is needed that we are superior…

🐱 CATS	🐶 DOGS
Are in charge.	Would come running if a human called to them, 'Over here, Mr Thickie!'
Are clean.	If dogs cleaned themselves with their tongues, their tongues would fall off and then germinate into hideous tongue trees, which would be poisonous. Humans would use them in chemical warfare and everyone would die.
Know that silence is golden.	Bark at absolutely anything, itching for a scrap. They even bark at cars. I dream that one day a car will square up to a dog – then we'll see who would win.
Eat only the choicest foods.	Consider an overturned bin to be an invitation to a dinner party.

CATS | **DOGS**

See in colour.	See in black-and-white. Everything to them is a 1965 episode of *Lost in Space*, which is why they always look so confused.
Women like cats.	Men like dogs. Ruff said.

How To... Become Feral

Much is made of manners. Often too much. How come feral cats get to have all the fun? Out at all hours, singing and carousing! Not a care in the world! Ever feel you've been short-changed? No longer! Here is my step-by-step guide to a walk on the wild side.

1. Step out of your house. Leave a note saying, 'I ain't ever coming back!', which goes on to explain how you have felt like a prisoner in your own home and were never allowed to have any fun. That'll show 'em!

2. While you've only made it to the bottom of the garden and are wondering if it's actually safe to go any further (for about eight hours), ignore your family's pleas for you to return, shrug off their agonized cries. Stuff them!

3. Go on, you can do it! Walk out of your own garden into next door's. You're FREE! Yes, I know you're hungry – just focus on your new-found freedom.

4. As night falls – it's Party Time! Oh yes! All you need now are some other feral cats to party with. Listen for the sounds of caterwauling. Watch for the signs of cat campfires. Seen some? Good – now head towards the flames...

5. Yes, I know they look hard. That's their job – they're feral! What did you expect? What do you mean, you suddenly feel very tired? Feral cats stay up all night! They don't worry about sleepy-byes! Trust me: just go up to them and ask if you can join in their party. They'll be fine. That's it, go on...

6. Run! Run like the wind! Yes, they are gaining on you. Yes, that one's head has gone rotten. Run faster!

7. Dive through your catflap, wailing furiously! Your human servant should wake up, come downstairs all bleary-eyed and shoo those nasty feral cats away. He has? Good.

8. Now saunter past him, head in the air, pure contempt, as if he's completely ruined your fun – and if he expects you to eat all that food he's laying out for you, he's got another think coming. The git.

9. When he's gone back to bed, eat all the food. (Well, you are very hungry.)

10. Sleep for ages, my brave soldier.

Famous Cats in History

1. The Cat in the Hat

The Cat in the Hat is a creation of the writer/cartoonist Dr Seuss, whose story about the moggy became so popular it was later turned into a truly terrible film starring Mike Myers. Still the Cat in the Hat will go down in history. And I wondered: why?

What if the Cat in the Hat hadn't had a hat? What if he was just The Cat? Doesn't sound so very interesting any more, does he? Which means that it's the hat that made him famous! And I wondered: what if I bought myself a hat – could I be famous too?

So I picked up a hat at the local milliner's, added a few accessories and wandered out into the street wearing it, feeling all suave and important. My mistake. How was I to know the local townsfolk would be holding a Pour Abuse on Cats Day?

> So I shall never wear
> A hat
> Like that
> Shall I
>
> For the folk in town
> Stared down
> At me:
> The butcher
> The baker
> The builder
> The banker
> And all as one
> Called me a…
>
> Let's leave it there, shall we?

Purring - How It Works

Purring: the sound we cats make when we're happy. It's there because human servants hear it, imagine they're making themselves useful for once, so they carry on doing whatever it was that was making us happy. It seldom fails.

But how does purring work, you ask?

In each of our throats is a room containing oiled bees. Normally, the door to this room is closed and the oiled bees are asleep.

But when our vast cat brain tells us we are happy, it sends a janitor to wake up the bees. The synchronized beating of their oily wings then creates the melodious purring sound we cats are noted for.

However: a word of warning! (For the human servants, not us.) Once woken, the oiled bees like to exercise their wings for at least half an hour. Anything less, and they get angry. Anything far less, and they might well stream out of their cat's mouth to sting the human servant to death! (True!)

So next time your human servant stops scratching you under the chin after just 15 or 20 minutes, let them heed our warning. And woe betide those lazy serfs.

Famous Cat Lovers 1

Florence Nightingale had so many kittens and cats she didn't know what to do. That must be why she always worked with one 'tied in a knot round her neck' (where was the Cats Protection League?). Her moggies were called embarrassing things like Tib, Mrs Tit and Poor Mr Muff which could be why so many went AWOL. Perhaps it was catching. The Lady with the Lamp lived next door to Lord Lucan and he hasn't been back in a while either.

Things for Cats to Build:

1. Rapport with Soft Furnishings

This is Lesson One in any decent manual of kitten raising. Every self-respecting mother cat should teach her children this at the earliest possible opportunity.

YOU WILL NEED:

- Large tool box
- Some materials (wood, whatever)
- Matches
- Kitten's father asleep on gilded sofa.

INSTRUCTIONS:

Mother cat, look your kittens in the eye. Let them know how serious this lesson is. That if they learn nothing else ever, this will still stand them in good stead for the rest of their lives.

1. Lay out some tools from the tool box and place the materials beside them. Explain to your children what hard work is: that it involves arduous labour, sweat and exertion for many hours, and that the reward is in the pride of seeing something they themselves have created.

2. Laugh! Laugh heartily! Laugh until your sides ache!

3. Now use the matches! Burn that tool box, its tools and all those materials! Let your young ones take in this scene. Hopefully, they will understand in an instant; however, they may well be very confused.

4. Now explain to them that cats don't do hard work. They get their human servants to do it for them, by wheedling around them in a variety of ways (see: 'How To… Wheedle Around Your Human Servants', page 18). If your kittens still seem unconvinced, go to 5.

5. Point to their father, asleep on a gilded sofa. Explain that doing naff all has got him everywhere, not forgetting the fact that his life is one long nap, punctuated only by mollycoddling and free food.

6. Place your kittens gently next to their father on the sofa and allow them time to enjoy its gentle embrace. Have they fallen asleep? Good.

7. Your work is done here. You deserve a long nap and some free food.

Why Aren't Cats 'Man's Best Friend'?

It's an outrage! A blatant and very cruel case of reverse discrimination. What was 'man' thinking?! I mean, who's the best out of cats and dogs? It's really no contest, is it? Let's see…

> ## THE THINGS DOGS ARE GOOD AT:
>
> - Fetching things
> - Being subservient
> - Smelling
> - Drooling.

THE THINGS CATS ARE GOOD AT:

Everything bar the above.

Which would you choose? I mean, why would any human servant... Hmm, I suppose treating humans as our servants isn't all that endearing.

But why would any human servant want a smelly, drooling creature around them who bends to their will... Hmm.

But why would any human servant want a smelly, drooling creature around them who bends to their will, is ceaselessly obedient, fiercely loyal, devotedly friendly, not afraid of hard work... Hmm.

But why would any human servant want a smelly, drooling creature around them who bends to their will, is ceaselessly obedient, fiercely loyal, devotedly friendly, not afraid of hard work, dependable in a crisis, protects them against any enemy... Look, I think we'll leave it there.

I simply say again: Why aren't cats 'Man's Best Friend'?! It's an outrage!

Famous Cat Lovers 2
Isaac Newton wasn't the brightest spark – he was the chump who sat in an orchard with apples bouncing off his bonce – but he did invent one useful thing, the cat flap. He wore it on his head and every lady and gentleman he passed paused to admire his fabulous new headwear. 'My, Mr Newton, how suave you look!' they said... Hang on a sec, I'm getting confused with flat caps.

Cat Personalities

Cats have uniquely wonderful and varied characteristics. According to the experts, there are no fewer than five types of cat personality commonly in existence. These are:

1. Vain
2. Crotchety
3. Spiteful
4. Slothful
5. Great

I'm sure you can guess which category I come under, readers. But how can you spot other personality types? Here are the telltale signs:

1. The vain cat...

- Glues self to minor celebrities' shoulders, to ensure being photographed by paparazzi.
- Seems terribly keen on the local Mirror & Glass shop.
- Self-publishes own *My Story* biography, then buys all copies to make it look popular.

2. The crotchety cat...

- Wears T-shirt bearing slogan: 'It's not PMT – I'm like this all the time.'
- Rips off his T-shirt and burns it, having suddenly become annoyed by slogan.
- Often spotted furiously crossing out all the minims and quavers in sheet music.

3. The spiteful cat...

- Hisses at inanimate objects.
- Practises scratching eyes out on teddy bears.
- Other cats give such a wide berth, tends to be the only cat for miles around.

4. The slothful cat...

- Usually surrounded by sloths, who mistake for one of their own species; when they realize their error, they take weeks to run away.
- Such cats congregate at STOP signs, using that as excuse.
- Can be too lazy to walk to the food bowl, has been known to train ants to bring bowl to him.

5. The great cat...

- Name of Al.
- That's him pictured at the front of this book.
- Breathes on claws, polishes on his chest fur.

Cats in Film

Being gorgeous and the brightest creatures to walk the Earth, it's no wonder that cats have been the stars of many a great movie. Here are just a few:

CAT ON A HOT TIN ROOF

A cat sits on a hot tin roof, finds it a tad uncomfortable and moves to a small wooden bench. Wood, being a poorer conductor of heat than metal, is cooler. The cat is happy. And that's good enough for me.

THE LION, THE WITCH AND THE WARDROBE

There's a lion, a witch and a wardrobe (which should have been obvious from the title, which lacks a certain imagination). The lion and the witch enjoy a nice chat; the wardrobe just sits there. No manners, no social graces, no wit, nothing. Eventually, the wardrobe pipes up: 'Hey, the lion and the witch,' he says. 'Walk into me and you could enter the magical world of Narnia!'

'What's Narnia?' asks the lion.

'Don't ask me,' says the wardrobe. 'I'm only a wardrobe.'

BLOFELD'S CAT IN THE JAMES BOND FILMS

Bald bloke with vivid scar sits in big chair, owns cat, wants to destroy the world. James Bond defeats Blofeld by blowing up a big mountain hideout or similar. However, the cat survives, since he was out on the tiles at the time.

THE TRUTH ABOUT CATS AND DOGS

Cats are great. Dogs are plop-plops. The End.

CAT PEOPLE

Some humans think they're cats. They aren't.
Definitely not. Cats are far superior.

CATWOMAN

Plot: by day, Logan Berry is a mild-mannered secretary; by
night, she dons a PVC catsuit with pointy ears and imagines
she is Catwoman. Logan has a history of mental illness.

(Not So) Famous Cat Lovers 3

Rutherford B Hayes was the 19th president
of the US of A but few remember him. Hardly
surprising. When presented with the first
Siamese cat in the USA, he responded by calling
her Miss Pussy. Was that the best he could do?
It's wrong that cats have never been allowed
into politics. Cats would instantly stop war, end
global warming and fairly distribute the wealth
of each nation. (Hmm, maybe not.)

When Cats Go Missing

You'd be amazed at how many cats have second homes, do a bit of moonlighting on the side or travel the country attending national events. This can, sadly, lead to confusion all round.

It's heartbreaking when a cat goes missing, and their human servants pin up notices around town: 'MISSING – Tabby cat named Fluffy. Reward offered.' That type of thing.

But: spot that 'Reward offered' bit.

I've thought up a cunning way to exploit the situation. Gather your mates together and, once you've stopped fighting, agree a plan. One of you has to Go Missing. For a few days. Their human servants will be distraught, but that only serves them right because we cats deserve only the very best and they were no doubt falling some distance short on that score.

Hide under a hedge, and when you hear the human servants calling out the missing cat's name – 'Here, Tiddles! Here, Tiddles' – snigger a lot, but not so loudly that they hear.

Eventually they'll put their hands in their wallets – the tight gits – and post up those notices, offering a reward. Here's where it gets tricky. What human is going to hand cash over to a cat? But I've had a brainwave: five cats, standing on each other's shoulders, wearing a raincoat and a hat.

Ring on the doorbell, the 'missing' cat is reunited with its owner, the human hands over lots of lovely cash and we go spend it on cat treats! Bob's your uncle.

Dear Cat Psychiatrist

My human servants keep laughing at me.
Yours, Tiddles.

Dear Tiddles
What do you expect when you're named after weeing? Get a proper name! Sheesh.
C.P.

THE CAT PSYCHIATRIST IS **IN**

Spraying - An Alternative

Cats mark out their territory, that's just a fact of life. However, some human servants don't take kindly to us weeing all over the place. Talk about picky.

As a compromise, I have come up with a solution which allows us cats to continue to spray, as nature intended, while removing the nasty odour.

Now everyone's happy! (I'm a genius.)

Why Cats Have Nine Lives

In case you hadn't noticed, it's perilous out there in the big, wide world – especially when we're sharing it with humans. Far too many of them are dangerous nutters. Consider these true stories:

BALDWIN III, COUNT OF YPRES

In AD926, Baldwin III – they named two other kids Baldwin?! – the Count of Ypres in Belgium, decided it would be a perfectly wonderful whizz to lob a load of cats off the 70-metre-high Cloth Tower. To see how they managed to survive long drops. Cheers for that.

This tradition continued until 1817, when one town official noted that the cat in question 'ran off quickly so that it might never be caught again in a similar ceremony'. Paws up, anyone who's surprised!

ETIENNE-JULES MAREY

You'd have thought that would be an end to such experiments. Alas no. Not for physiologist/ photographer Etienne-Jules Marey anyway. In 1894, he filmed cats falling off tall buildings, to see how they righted themselves.

If he'd only asked, we could have told him! It's just a shame he didn't try throwing himself off the same tall building, to see whether landing on one's feet would work for humans. 'What was that, Etienne-Jules? I can't understand you – try taking your mouth out of your shoes.'

As if that wasn't enough, humans used to brick cats up in the walls of houses, to ward off evil spirits. Honestly. WHO FIRST CAME UP WITH THAT WIZARD WHEEZE?

> COMPLETE IDIOT: 'I think we've got evil spirits. I know – let's brick Felix up in the dining-room wall! Yes, that should do the trick!'
>
> *Later...*
>
> EVIL SPIRIT 1: 'I've just been mooching around the cavity walls, moaning a bit, and you'll never guess what – I found a cat in there!'
>
> EVIL SPIRIT 2: 'A cat? In the cavity walls? I hate cats in cavity walls! Quick, let's get out of here!'

Not a terribly realistic scenario, is it?

And that's the sort of thing we cats have had to put up with throughout history. Quite apart from the modern threats of being bored to death, riddled with obesity or stuffed into microwaves by teenagers.

Nine lives? It ain't enough.

> ### HERE ARE JUST SOME OF THE WAYS IN WHICH I AND SOME OF MY CAT FRIENDS HAVE LOST LIVES:
>
> **1.** I once went parachuting off the shed roof. Big mistake. Dented my pride, ripped my human servants' best winceyette sheet and then they dragged me spitting and spewing into the bath after I ended up in the septic tank. (What made them put a thing like that there?)
>
> **2.** My mate Felix forgot to turn off the chip pan after he had murdered 12 pints down the local pub. Singed his fur and barely made it through the catflap into the garden. The owners of his house weren't too chuffed either.

3. A good friend of mine, Chester, took a nap in a tumble dryer. Not the safest place for forty winks.

4. And his mate Dave, who's allergic to nuts, failed to realize that satay sauce is peanut-based. Mind you, Dave's so thick, he didn't even know that peanut butter is peanut-based. And peanuts! (God rest his soul!)

5. I once climbed a tree. No problem there, you might think, but never again shall I wonder what a sign saying, 'Tree Felling in Progress' means.

6. Marge the Manx cat had high-rise syndrome. She slipped from her windowsill at the very top of a tall block of flats, just a split second before her human servant lunged to catch her. If only she'd had a tail…

7. Never bite into electric cable, sleep under a parked car or get stuck down a well. We've all been there…

8. Fish bone stuck in the throat. It's happened to the best of us.

9. I once did several energetic things in one day. The exertion proved too much for my system. Never again. (Heed that one well, my feline friends.)

Famous Cats in History

2. Dick Whittington's Cat

The folk tale goes – yes, it was a proper story before it became a pantomime – that Dick Whittington travelled to London to make his fortune, after people round his way had told him that the city's streets were 'paved with gold'.

It's just an expression, dummy – you're not meant to take it literally! But Thickie Dickie's down on his hands and knees inspecting the pavement, thinking to himself, 'Looks like stone to me.'

He ends up being taken in by a kindly merchant named Fitzwarren, who takes pity on the grovelling idiot. Whittington is given a job as Fitzwarren's scullery boy and is offered a room in the house – which is overrun with rats. (Kinda puts that previous 'kindly' into perspective, doesn't it?)

Enter Dick Whittington's cat. Some sanity at last. The cat scares off all the rats and Dick can sleep soundly at night. How can such bravery be repaid? Dick gives the cat to Fitzwarren, who makes a load of cash selling him to the King of Barbary, whose palace is infested with mice.

Dick becomes Mayor of London – I missed some of the story out there – and everyone lives happily ever after. Except the cat, who can't speak Barbarian and has grown sick to death of the all-mouse diet.

That's how the human version of the tale goes. Of course, it's pure unadulterated tosh. Who really wore the trousers in the Whittington household? I'll give you a clue: here's what the story should actually have been titled…

Cat's Dick Whittington

…And this version is a lot shorter. It goes like this:

Whittington comes to London with cat.

Whittington becomes frantic cross-dresser.

On account of this, curious people tend to follow him around, sniggering.

Others point this out to Whittington with cries of 'He's behind you!'

Cat spots potential for lame entertainment and invents 'pantomime'.

The End.

'Oh no, it isn't!' Etc.

'See, I've Climbed This Tree By Mistake...'

We all get a little adventurous, particularly during our kitten years. However, one fact remains: cats aren't supposed to climb trees. No way. Does that stop some of us? No, it doesn't.

Let's put the silliness aside now and focus on the practicality. What should you do if you've climbed a tree by mistake? You're up there amid the top branches and suddenly becoming the next Edmund Hillary has lost all of its appeal. Your nerve has deserted you but you're too scared to climb down. Genius.

Right. There's nothing for it but to mewl pathetically, as loud as you can. Cats can't help you now. You need some human servants, preferably a dear old lady with a bag. So here are your instructions:

1. Mewl as if your life depends upon it (since it does).

2. Once you've attracted the dear old lady with a bag's attention – avoid youths in hoods, who will only throw stones and find your predicament briefly hilarious, before slouching off to the nearest shopping centre – keep mewling.

3. She will call up at you, somehow imagining that you understand human. 'Are you stuck?' 'Come on, kitty, you can climb down!' – that type of nonsense. Ignore her and hope she locates someone more useful to ask for their help.

4. When the more useful person arrives, they will both stare up at you, probably pointing. Others may gather with them. It's all right, they know you're there now; you can safely revert to ignoring them as if they are dirt.

5. You may hear sirens – a good sign – or a fire engine might just turn up unannounced. This is the Fire Service. They have ladders, which is just the job.

6. A fireman will climb a very high ladder, risking life and limb to reach you. Try to scratch his eyes out when he gets there. (It's only fair.)

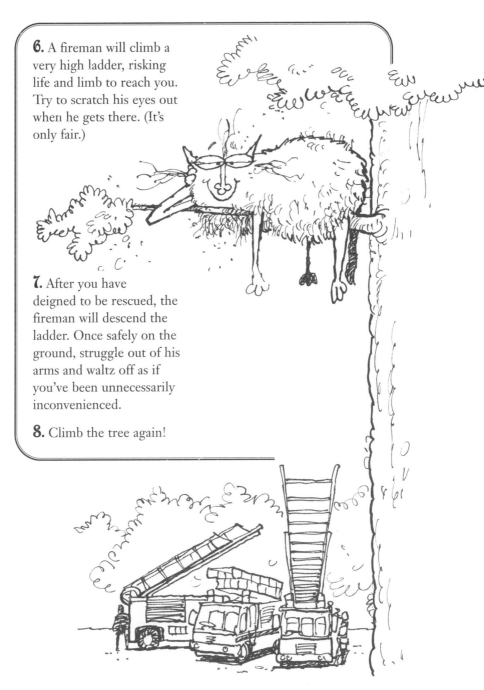

7. After you have deigned to be rescued, the fireman will descend the ladder. Once safely on the ground, struggle out of his arms and waltz off as if you've been unnecessarily inconvenienced.

8. Climb the tree again!

If Only They'd Invented...

Here are some innovations I consider would make cats' hard lives so very much easier. (Why have so many boffins been wasting their lives on other matters?) I only wish someone had invented the following...

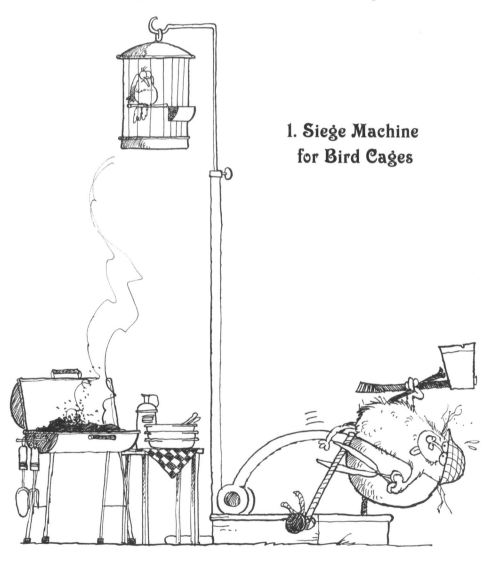

1. Siege Machine for Bird Cages

2. Deep Sea Diving Suit for Cats

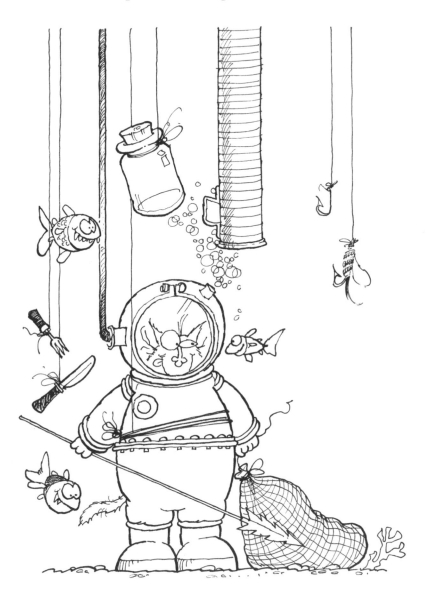

3. Collar Removal Stations

4. Mouse Trap

Sorry? Mouse traps already exist? So why am I still doing all the work?!

Famous Cat Lovers 4

What was going on in the twisted mind of
Edgar Allan Poe? 'The Black Cat' is about a
man who tortures his cat and then kills his wife.
Elsewhere, Poe's cats are symbols of evil. In real
life, he lived with a cat called Catarina. During
the terrible winter of 1846 when his wife was
dying of TB, this noble creature slept with her
to keep her warm. Where is the gratitude?

Games Cats Can Play

1. Fetch

Let's be frank here, this is more one for dogs, but that doesn't stop some of our human servants from trying. It can be ultra-tedious when humans have foolishly selected the wrong breed of animal. Here's how to cope.

If your human servant is throwing something they're hoping you'll fetch for them, you'll know about it because they get all excited. They'll keep looking from you to the object and back, eyebrows raised, urging you, 'Go on – fetch it!' or something dumb like that.

Ignore them. If you're not already lying down, do so.

The chances are they will persist. (In human servant terms it's known as 'training' – fascism by another name. Cats cannot be 'trained'.)

Resist any urge to lunge at the object, just to shut them up. Instead, look them in the eye every now and again – this will get their hopes up. (Heheh.)

Now walk away.

Repeat this process every time a game of Fetch is on the cards. Walk away, walk away, walk away.

Eventually your human servant will realize you have no interest in fetching anything and will give up on the game. (In cat terms this is known as 'training' – altruism by another name. Humans *can* be 'trained'.)

Cat The Ripper

Cats kill 50 million small animals every year in Britain alone. Murder, maim, eviscerate. It's what we do. It's why human servants began keeping us as 'pets' – silly word – at the very beginnings of civilization: to bump off the vermin.

Are we appreciated for it? No. (Some human servants even attach silver bells to our collars as if we are lepers, so everyone can hear us coming. Next they'll be expecting us to put on gloves and a red cloak, and to go round muttering, 'Unclean! Unclean!')

Are we appreciated for anything, really? Indeed no.

What are we going to do about it? Go on strike? Have our claws removed! Do community service for rodents? In fact, I'd go further. Let's start holding wine and cheese parties for all the local mice!

Our human servants will soon get the message, and start treating us with a little respect. After which all those bloated, tipsy little morsels will be a doddle to catch…

Famous Cat Haters 1

Ghengis Khan, Alexander the Great, Julius Caesar, Napoleon, Mussolini and Hitler. What links them? Yes, I know they twonked thousands of humans, but the answer I'm looking for is that each of them had ailurophobia – a posh Greek word for fear of cats. None of them could bear to be in our regal presence. Small animals suffer from the same mental illness. What should they do? Well, I'd begin running if I were them… it's much more fun when you give them a start.

The Legendary Cats' Chorus

The thing is, some of you might be thinking to yourselves, 'Lordy, no, not that cacophonous racket! Not at this time of night.' But it wasn't always thus. There was a time…

When, around the mid-18th century, famous composer Johann Sebastian Bach was looking to recruit singers for his regular Christmas Oratorio, a bunch of cats wandered into his studio and began to sing. And such a lovely noise did they make, that Bach, whose sight was well iffy, employed them as his chorus on the spot. This was the original Cats' Chorus.

Why did these assembled moggies make such a delightful noise? Three reasons:

1. They gargled with castor oil before they went to bed.

2. They loved music and were always listening in from the windowsills of the great composers.

3. They practised a lot in karaoke bars.

Of course, when Bach's advisers came in, they would say to the great man, 'You do know you've employed a load of alley cats and strays, don't you?' And he would wave them away and say, 'Nonsense! And even if it were true, these alley cats and strays have sweeter voices than the sweetest human voices of our generation.' (It's possible he was also going a bit deaf like so many old composers.)

Anyway, the audiences of the day, desperate to be seen as fashionable, latched on to this idea of the Cats' Chorus so they were feted wherever they went. Flowers were thrown on to the stage, and occasionally ladies' underwear, which was voluminous back in those days, and so could be sold to parachute-makers after the concerts to make a few extra bob.

Bach's contemporaries – Vivaldi, Scarlatti, Handel, Rameau – came to hear about Bach's sell-out performances and became insanely jealous. Suddenly they all wanted a feline-based choral company, too.

Vivaldi wrote his 'Concerto for Cats and a Lute in B Minor', Scarlatti premiered his 'Felinio Operetta', Handel composed his 'Hair on a Cat Blanket' – and Rameau penned his jingle for the Miaow Mix advert, which went:

'Miaow-miaow-miaow-miaow miaow-miaow-miaow-miaow miaow-miaow-miaow-miaow miaow-miaow-miaow-miaow' [etc. – you get my drift].

Which proved too much for the refined ears of the age.

'What's Miaow Mix, anyway?' they enquired.

And so the Cats' Choruses were kicked out into the streets and composers went back to people with lovely voices.

(I'd rather listen to a kitten going 'miaow' repeatedly than some busty bint warbling about princes, any day. But there's no accounting for taste.)

Cats in Animation

Cats are terribly popular in animation, and I did wonder why. (I really did.) Then I heard the animators thinking out aloud to themselves, 'Which is the world's most beautiful creature, yet has wit and warmth and modesty in spades?' And the reason leapt out at me.

Tom

TENDENCIES: To try to catch Jerry (a mouse, lest we forget) in a variety of imaginative, colourful and eye-catching ways.

WHY IT'S CLEARLY A CARTOON: The mouse always wins and Tom has been known to swallow an iron, an event he would be unlikely to survive in real life.

TYPICAL STORYLINE: Tom sets a trap for Jerry, which the dog Spike falls for instead. Spike duffs Tom's head in.

TYPICAL QUOTE: It's more of a scream, really. Sort of 'AAAAAAAAGH!'

IS HE FUNNY? Sure, but where's the pride?

Top Cat/Boss Cat

TENDENCIES: To pull a fast one on the human characters.

WHY IT'S CLEARLY A CARTOON: Sounds like real life to me.

TYPICAL STORYLINE: Officer Dibble tries to evict Top Cat and gang from their alleyway, and fails.

TYPICAL QUOTE: All right, it's more the theme tune, but I bet you never realized the lyrics went like this: 'Top Cat / The most effectual Top Cat / Whose intellectual close friends get to call him TC / Providing it's with dignity…' I thought it went: 'Top Cat / The most effectual Top Cat / Whose intellectual close friends get to call him TC / Roma why ends licking the tea.' Admittedly their version makes more sense.

IS HE FUNNY? Am I gorgeous? (That's a yes, in case you're trying to be clever.)

Garfield

TENDENCIES: To lie around being fat and smug.

WHY IT'S CLEARLY A CARTOON:
Since when have you known cats to be smug?

TYPICAL STORYLINE: Garfield tries to steal a pie.

TYPICAL QUOTE:
'I love the smell of Cinnamon Apple in the morning.'

IS HE FUNNY? About as funny as waking up next to an eel in curlers. (Actually, not as funny as that.) The *LA Times* called the Garfield movie a 'soulless excuse for entertainment'.

Sylvester

TENDENCIES: To fail to catch Tweetie Pie, usually involving him being crushed by an Acme-branded anvil.

WHY IT'S CLEARLY A CARTOON: Acme don't make anvils.

TYPICAL STORYLINE: Sylvester pops his clogs. (Sylvester, whose full name is Sylvester J Pussycat Sr, has died more times than any other Looney Tunes character. True!)

TYPICAL QUOTE: From the episode, 'The Scarlet Pumpernickel': 'Firtht, I am happy, for I am to wed the Fair Melitha, then I am furiouth, becauthe I dethpithe the Thcarlet Puh... Puh... Puh... Pumpernickel!' (Sylvester has a lisp, those aren't typos.)

Felix

TENDENCIES: To go hungry (see: 'Felix Goes Hungry').

WHY IT'S CLEARLY A CARTOON: Since when did a cat go hungry? We're far too conniving for that.

TYPICAL STORYLINE: Felix asks this guy for a job the guy says he doesn't have any work for cats Felix runs off steals some cheese shows the cheese to a load of mice who then follow him back to the guy's place Felix lobs the cheese into the guy's house the mice dive in after it the guy begs Felix to stay. I hope you got all that.

TYPICAL QUOTE: '   ' (they were silent movies).

IS HE FUNNY? Judging by the above, no.

Shere Khan

TENDENCIES: To think he's great.

WHY IT'S CLEARLY A CARTOON: Just as bears don't indulge in song and dance routines, tigers don't talk with a plum in the mouth; they're more the rip-your-head-off-with-one-swipe type of creature.

TYPICAL STORYLINE: In *The Jungle Book* by Rudyard Kipling, Shere Khan (a lame tiger) tries to kill Mowgli, who has been adopted by wolves. He is then run over by buffalos and skinned by the boy. Disney failed to go with that storyline for some reason.

TYPICAL QUOTE: 'What beastly luck!' (Disney's Shere Khan attended public school and was expelled for bullying.)

IS HE FUNNY? Do bears sing in the woods?

Things for Cats to Build

2. Scratching Pole

e all love a scratching pole, don't we? Sharpen those claws, work off a little aggression. Keep those abs and pecs in top condition. Here's how to make one.

YOU WILL NEED:

- Thick wooden pole
- Square wooden base
- Rope
- Furry ball on string
- Carpet tile
- Glue
- Human servant.

INSTRUCTIONS:

Show your human servant these instructions. They are quite easy to follow. Paw at them, purr and rub yourself against your human servant's legs, until they realize what you're after. Now sit back and watch (or just have a nap, if you prefer).

1. Get your human servant to glue the carpet tile to the square wooden base, then screw the thick wooden pole to the base so it stands upright. Wind the rope tightly around the pole, gluing in place. Like this:

2. To finish the project off – since one should take pride in one's work – the human servant should glue the furry ball on string to the top of the pole. Purely an extra plaything, since we need all the entertainment we can get.

3. Nice work! Have another nap and some free food!

Some Things a Cat Might Eat

I t's a spiteful myth that cats are excessively choosy. In fact they will eat most things a reasonable-minded human servant will set in front of them, including the following:

- 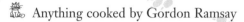 Anything cooked by Gordon Ramsay

- Or Marco Pierre White

- Or Mario Batali

- But not that Jamie Oliver bloke – his outsized tongue puts me off

- Oysters? Maybe, but only with a dash of fresh lime juice and a hint of tabasco

- Truffles? Nah. Too mushroom-y

- Pâté de foie gras? Bleugh. Rubbish. I wouldn't feed that to a dog.

- Exquisite sashimi prepared by Japan's most celebrated chef? You're kidding! If I want a teeny weeny portion of masterfully sliced fish, I'll ask for it!

Dear Cat Psychiatrist
Everyone thinks I'm a compulsive liar. Yours, Kitty.

Dear Kitty
I don't believe a word
of it.
C. 'Boom Boom' P.

THE CAT PSYCHIATRIST IS **IN**

I find it hilarious how desperate our human servants are to please our palates. Play up to it.

HERE'S HOW TO APPROACH
A BOWL OF FOOD:

1. Regard the proffered delicacy as if it were something you brought in on your back paw.

2. Sniff at it with all the enthusiasm of a turkey waking up to the words, 'Oooh, it's Christmas Eve!'

3. Walk away.

4. Witness your human servant being distraught. Good. Serves them right.

5. When they're not looking, nip back and wolf the lot down.

Famous Cats in History

3. Teddy Roosevelt's Cat, Slippers

American presidents are famous for keeping cats in the White House. Rutherford B Hayes owned the nation's first-ever Siamese cat; Jimmy Carter's daughter, Amy, owned any number of felines, including a Siamese she named – alarmingly – Misty Malarky Ying Yang; and Abraham Lincoln first started the trend with his cat, Tabby. Guess what colour that was? You'd think that people that important could find some sort of happy medium between Tabby and Misty Malarky Ying Yang. Anyway.

Actually, while we're on the subject of presidents' pets, Woodrow Wilson kept a ram on the White House lawn, which is said to have chewed tobacco, William Taft owned a cow, named Pauline Wayne, and James Buchanan had a herd of elephants! (True! The madness!)

President Edward Roosevelt – famous also for inventing teddy bears and the electric tin opener – had a cat called Slippers. Slippers had too many toes, which made him a pterodactyl.

Hang on, let me check that again. Sorry, it's polydactyl. So Slippers had too many toes – more than five on each foot – which is not hugely uncommon in the cat world. I have 77 toes, but don't like to boast.

Why was Slippers named Slippers, you may ask. Well, let's just assume that you did. Look, I'm not going to argue with you. Slippers was called Slippers because President Roosevelt was rather short-sighted and each morning when he woke up, he looked down at the side of his bed where the cat habitually slept – and thought he was one of his slippers!

The president would then happily wander down to breakfast, where he would read the morning paper and chew on his toast until one of the maids pointed out that he had a cat on his foot. Other than that, he was excellent at running the country and much loved.

Indeed, our Teddy fancied himself as a bit of a Noah. Not content with keeping a cat, he actually ran his own mini-zoo. Besides Slippers, the Roosevelt family also owned (this, too, is all true):

- Thirteen horses (Bleistein, Renown, Roswell, Rusty, Jocko, Root, Grey, Dawn, Wyoming, Yangenka, General, Judge, Algonquian)

- Five dogs (Pete, Sailor Boy, Jack, Skip, Manchu)

- Various snakes (one named Emily Spinach)

- One macaw (Eli Yale)

- Another cat (Tom Quartz)

- A badger (Josiah)

- Five guinea pigs (Dewey Senior, Dewey Junior, Bob Evans, Bishop Doan, Father O'Grady)

- One lion

- One hyena

- One wildcat

- Five bears

- Two parrots

- One zebra

- One barn owl

- Lizards

- Rats

- Roosters

- And a raccoon.

How Slippers managed to survive, I have no idea.

(**Author's note**: British Prime Minster Winston Churchill also owned a cat, a ginger tabby, who was named Jock. Jock shared Churchill's bed and the great man also took him to wartime cabinet meetings. It is rumoured that the D-Day landings were Jock's idea, but the suggestion was covered up in case the British people worried that the nation's battle strategies were being proposed by a cat. How very narrow-minded.)

Big Cats - Are They Really So Scary?

Yes!

Spot the difference

Cat Horoscopes

The skies show the path ahead for each one of us. Ever wondered what the stars hold in store for you? Now's your chance to find out with our amazing guest astrologer, Mystic Mogg.

CAPRICORN (22 DEC – 20 JAN)

PERSONALITY TRAITS: Can be a bit boring

LIKES: Knitting hats for the homeless, debating tensile strength of girders

DISLIKES: Fancy-dress parties

MOST LIKELY TO SAY: 'My, that girder looks sturdy!'

LEAST LIKELY TO SAY: 'Actually, girders are rather boring – shall we talk about something else?'

FAVOURITE FOOD: Frog pâté

AQUARIUS (20 JAN – 19 FEB)

PERSONALITY TRAITS: Breaks into song at the drop of a hat

LIKES: Psychoanalysis, and pushing hat wearers into wind tunnels

DISLIKES: Hat pins

MOST LIKELY TO SAY: 'The hills are alive with the sound of music!'

LEAST LIKELY TO SAY: 'I can't be doing with that Michael Ball nonsense.'

FAVOURITE FOOD: Caviar and chips

PISCES (20 FEB – 20 MAR)

PERSONALITY TRAITS: Prone to lethargy, loves fish

LIKES: Sleeping

DISLIKES: Being woken up

MOST LIKELY TO SAY: 'Zzzzzzzzzzzzzz.'

LEAST LIKELY TO SAY: 'Right, what's first on the agenda?'

FAVOURITE FOOD: Anything prepared to crawl into mouth

ARIES (21 MAR – 20 APR)

PERSONALITY TRAITS: Bit of a snob

LIKES: The works of Gustav Mahler

DISLIKES: Being drawn into discussions about The Spice Girls

MOST LIKELY TO SAY: 'I find the counterpoint exquisite, darling!'

LEAST LIKELY TO SAY: 'Zig-a-zig-ah.'

FAVOURITE FOOD: Canapés

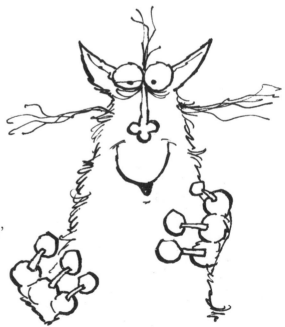

TAURUS (21 APR – 21 MAY)

PERSONALITY TRAITS: Bullish

LIKES: Running after Spaniards

DISLIKES: Red rags

MOST LIKELY TO SAY: 'Gimme that!'

LEAST LIKELY TO SAY: 'Would you mind if…'

FAVOURITE FOOD: Yours

GEMINI (22 MAY – 21 JUN)

PERSONALITY TRAITS: Enjoys being the centre of attention

LIKES: Cravats, monocles and crisp whisker arrangements

DISLIKES: Other cats

MOST LIKELY TO SAY: 'I couldn't possibly! Oh, go on then.'

LEAST LIKELY TO SAY: 'After you!'

FAVOURITE FOOD: Double cream (sterilized)

CANCER (22 JUN – 23 JUL)

PERSONALITY TRAITS: Fatalistic

LIKES: Seances

DISLIKES: The manufacturing process behind blue cheese

MOST LIKELY TO SAY: 'We'll all be dead soon anyway.'

LEAST LIKELY TO SAY: 'My favourite cheese? Stilton, probably.'

FAVOURITE FOOD: Hedgehog sandwich

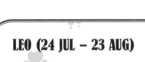

LEO (24 JUL – 23 AUG)

PERSONALITY TRAITS:
Lets the wife do
all the work

LIKES: Lying under
trees and getting as
drunk as a lord

DISLIKES: Gazelles

MOST LIKELY TO SAY: 'I'll scratch yer eyes out!'

LEAST LIKELY TO SAY: 'No, no, let me get that.'

FAVOURITE FOOD: Organic Gravadlax

VIRGO (24 AUG – 23 SEP)

PERSONALITY TRAITS: Can be rather wishy-washy

LIKES: Enunciating the word 'tragic'

DISLIKES: Being told to pay attention

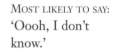

MOST LIKELY TO SAY: 'Oooh, I don't know.'

LEAST LIKELY TO SAY: 'I'll sort this out!'

FAVOURITE FOOD: Fresh farm milk

LIBRA (24 SEP – 23 OCT)

PERSONALITY TRAITS: Never happy

LIKES: Standing up for the underdog

DISLIKES: Autumn fashions

MOST LIKELY TO SAY: 'Do you like my wig?'

LEAST LIKELY TO SAY: 'I'm sure he didn't mean it.'

FAVOURITE FOOD: Foie gras on slivers of dodo

SCORPIO (24 OCT – 22 NOV)

PERSONALITY TRAITS: Easily confused

LIKES: The smell of bacon

DISLIKES: Eggs

MOST LIKELY TO SAY: 'I have a breakfast quandary.'

LEAST LIKELY TO SAY: 'Two eggs, please.'

FAVOURITE FOOD: Bacon

SAGITTARIUS (23 NOV – 21 DEC)

PERSONALITY TRAITS: Overly philosophical

LIKES: Fishing for compliments

DISLIKES: Rash decisions

MOST LIKELY TO SAY: 'Que sera!'

LEAST LIKELY TO SAY: 'Ah, let's just do it – hang the consequences.'

FAVOURITE FOOD: Babies

Things for Cats to Build

3. Sofa

We all love a sofa. Mmm… soft cushions. But does your sofa look in need of repair? Holes in the armrests? Stains on the fabric? Then why not build a new one? Or, in cat terms, why not buy a new one? (It's a lot easier – and cheaper, especially since it's not you paying.)

YOU WILL NEED:

- Human servant
- Human servant's credit card
- Sofa store.

INSTRUCTIONS:

Let your human servant know that they need a new sofa. Some suggestions:

Turn your nose up every time they pat a cushion beside them and go, 'Come on! Come and sit with me!'

Pick at and sniff holes in fabric, wearing a snooty expression.

Plant a dead bird in the lining, claiming that you found it there and that it has been there all along.

If the above measures fail, pee all over it. That should do the trick. (If not, consider moving out.)

Now make sure your human servant buys a high-quality replacement, not any old foam-based tat. Here is my list of recommended outlets:

✔ **Catsco**

✔ **Miaowji**

✔ **Tabicat**

✔ **Sofas'ℜ'puss**

✔ **The FURniture Store**

✔ **The Argos CATalogue**

Definitely avoid these:

✘ **Littlewoofs**

✘ **Pribark**

✘ **eBark**

When your new sofa arrives, sit slap-bang in the middle of it and refuse to budge. Pretend to be asleep while chuckling inwardly at your human servants crammed on to the one you wee'd on!

Famous Cat Lovers 5

Many famous composers exploited cats remorselessly in their search for a tune you could hum. Frédéric Chopin took notes as his cat danced across the keyboard of his piano; it was the first run through of the 'Cat Waltz'. Scarlatti's kitty, Pulcinella, did a turn around the harpsichord to produce the Fugue in G Minor, L499, aka the 'Cat's Fugue'. But did either animal artist get royalties from these projects? Not on your nelly. Neither moggy saw a single red cent.

How To... Become a Cat Burglar

For some reason, humans can never have enough stuff, even if most of it is complete rubbish. Luckily, cats can help here. Stealing things is fun and it also helps keep the place tidy. Here's how:

1. Put on a stripey jumper (obligatory).

2. Carry a bag labelled 'SWAG' (also obligatory).

3. Sneak into a house.

4. Wonder what to steal, since most stuff in houses is pretty useless to us.

5. So just grab the nearest item to hand and scram. You don't want to get caught.

6. When you're back outside, think to yourself, 'Why have I just stolen a pedal bin? What's the point in that?' Well, you're stuck with it now!

7. Try to sell the pedal bin on the black market.

8. Wonder where the black market is.

9. Having trawled round all the markets you know, none of which are black, give up that idea.

10. Consider selling the pedal bin through a fence.

11. Find a fence with a hole in it and wait for buyers on the other side.

12. Realize there isn't much call for pedal bins being sold through fences.

13. How about trying Mr Big? He's always after stolen goods!

How do you get in touch? Look him up in the phone directory.

14. The nearest you can find is a Mrs Biggs. Ring her anyway.

15. Discover she doesn't need any stolen pedal bins, thank you very much.

16. Take off the stripey jumper, burn the bag labelled 'SWAG'.

17. Realize that a life of crime isn't for you.

18. Have a nap. You deserve it.

Famous Cats in History

4. Elsie

Elsie was a lioness who became famous for not eating this bloke who hung out with her, called Adam Joyson. Why didn't Elsie eat Adam? Or did she? It's a curious tale…

Adam Joyson was a naturist. Hang on, that's not right. Start again…

Adam Joyson was a naturalist. That's better. So, Adam Joyson was a naturalist who was particularly fond of big cats. However, as we know, big cats can be pretty tetchy and have large, sharp teeth and claws. They don't always take kindly to being disturbed by humans. Adam knew that if he wanted to study big cats in the wild, he would have to gain their trust. But how? You don't get second chances with big game, remember.

Adam used tried and tested cat psychology. He approached Elsie very slowly, holding out his hand and rubbing his fingers together as if he had food, while going, 'Here, kitty-kitty! Here, kitty-kitty!' And it seemed to work. Adam came within two or three yards of Elsie and she simply stared at him, probably thinking something along the lines of, 'What a twonk!'

Then she bit Adam's head off and ate him.

You'd think that was the end of the story. But it wasn't. Elsie started having pangs of guilt, particularly when a film crew turned up, muttering something about making a film called *Born Cheap*, about naturalists who make friends with lions. So Elsie knocked up a dummy in Adam's image, using some stuff she found in the bush: twigs and dead zebras, that sort of thing, which she dressed in Adam's clothes. And the film crew fell for it! Hook, line and sinker!

The film was a massive success and everyone lived happily ever after. (Adam Joyson notwithstanding.)

Famous Cat Lovers 6

The fortune teller Nostradamus lived with a cat called Grimalkin who was supposed to help him in the predictions game. Trouble is the old codger never listened to a word the cat said, which is why he got everything so badly wrong. It's a fact, cats are better at telling the future than humans: we can sense when an earthquake is about to rumble and, more importantly, where our next bowl of food is coming from. We're psychic like that!

Games Cats Can Play

2. Catch the Dangly String

I can only think that our human servants imagine we enjoy this game. Personally, I've never been more frustrated and bored in my entire life.

Lower the string...

We snatch at the string...

Pull up the string so we can't reach it...

Lower the string...

We snatch at the string...

Pull up the string so we can't reach it...

Lower the string...

We snatch at the string...

Pull up the string so we can't reach it...

Got it with a single claw! Tug! Nope,
they've pulled it away. Great...

Lower the string...

We snatch at the string...

Pull up the string so we
can't reach it...

It's worse than Chinese water torture!

So here's my plan to make sure they never try to play Catch the Dangly String again:

1. Get a load of mates round.

2. Hide them around the corner and tell them to keep quiet.

3. Wait until the bit in the game where you've snared the string with a single claw – now whistle to your mates.

4. All together now – heave!

5. Drag that human servant into a river!

6. Watch him float downstream from the safety of the bank.

7. Consider waving.

8. Go home.

Why Did the Cow Jump Over the Moon?

'Hey diddle-diddle, the cat and the fiddle, the cow jumped over the moon...'

Thus begins the nursery rhyme. But what the hell is it on about? And why did the cow jump over the moon, just because the cat had a fiddle? (The fiddle in question is a violin, by the way.)

The answer to the second question is easy. Have you ever heard fiddle music? Scratchity-scrape scrapity-iddle iddly-scratch, etc. It's like listening to 17 rats attempting to dance the can-can in a room full of polystyrene chips. You'd jump over the moon, too, just to escape it! (Which leaves the mystery of how the cow jumped over the moon – and I can explain that also. The cow had one of those jetpacks that James Bond used in *Thunderball*.)

As to the first question: what the hell is it on about? That's trickier. Nursery rhyme meanings often have their origins in a dark history, and should never be taken too literally.

'Ring-a-ring-a-roses', for instance, is all about the Black Death, not rings of roses. The final line, 'We all fall down', alludes to everyone dying of the Plague. Yes, it's a cheery number.

Another example: 'Jack and Jill went up the hill to fetch a pail of water...' – what could that mean? Jack and Jill represent the London Fire Brigade during the Great Fire of 1666. 'Jack fell down and broke his crown...'? Jack's fire helmet didn't have a regulation chin-strap, so it fell off in the confusion and Jack's head became trapped under a falling girder. 'And Jill came tumbling after...'? They were sexist times: women weren't deemed physically strong enough to cope with the rigours of fire-fighting. 'Jill came tumbling after'? Jill just fell over.

But what are we to make of 'The little dog laughed to see such fun/ And the dish ran away with the spoon'? And who wrote this crazy stuff in the first place?

Mother 'Ma' Goose, that's who, a notorious racketeer of the 17th century, who smuggled stolen pets into the Low Countries, did terrible things to kittens and ran a sideline in self-penned poetry.

These verses served a sinister double purpose: read by mothers to very young children, they also cunningly dispersed cryptic information to Goose's international network of fences, yeggs [robbers] and stool pigeons. Goose also authored the following sinister ditty: 'Cry, baby, cry?/ Put your finger in your eye/ And tell your mother it wasn't I.'

Yes, behind these apparently simple nursery rhymes lies a world of heartache and degradation.

Famous Cat Lovers 7 & 8

Ernest Hemingway called cats 'love sponges', something we won't go into now. One of his toms, Snowball, had six digits on each foot, experience of foreign travel as a ship's cat and a silver tongue – in short, he was every inch the ladies' man. You've got to hand it to the old boy. In Hemingway's Key West home, now a museum, he has over 60 descendants, each with 12 fine toes. That's the way we cats like to be remembered!!

Mark Twain wrote good things and bad. In the former category: 'If a man could be crossed with a cat, it would improve the man but deteriorate the cat.' He also said, 'If you hold a cat by the tail you learn things you cannot learn in any other way.' Try that on me, and he'd get a swift bunch of fives followed by a roadmap carved on his mush.

Hairless Cats

This is a hairless cat:

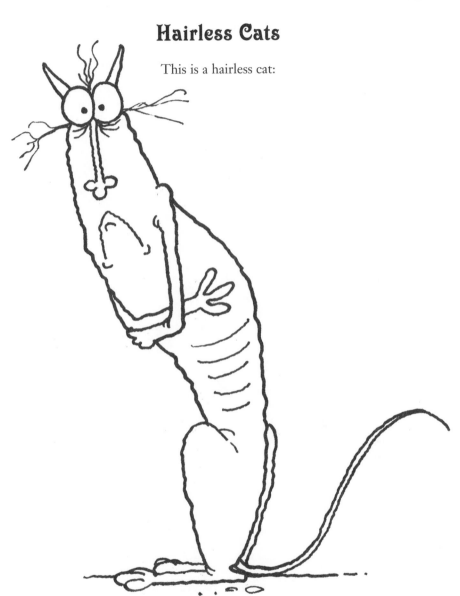

Just one question:
WHY?

The Lion King -
Well, I Didn't Vote for Him!

Anyone remember putting an X next to Simba's name and popping it into a polling box? Or Simba putting himself forward for king by travelling around in an open-top bus, shouting all the 'Friends, Romans, Countrymen' stuff through a megaphone, while wearing a big rosette with 'VOTE SIMBA FOR KING!' on it? Or even asking politely if we minded? Nope – me neither.

Where's the democracy in cat politics?!

But it's OK – I have a plan, my feline friends! I think I'd look quite good in a golden crown, so I'm going to put myself forward as a candidate for king in order to force an election. Then we'll see who everyone votes for! And unlike Simba, I have policies, my feline friends! [Thumps paw on lectern] I HAVE A MANIFESTO!

MY MANIFESTO

- Free food for all cats... Hang on, we get that already.

- The freedom to lounge around, whenever we wan... Hmm, and that.

- Cuddles, scratches, molly-codd... Right, yes.

- Say, our lives aren't so bad after all!

- There must be something else... I know! Since I get to wear a golden crown and wouldn't want anyone to feel left out: free nice hats for everyone else! Yes, that's it! Eat voting dust, Simba – the kingship is mine!

VOTE FOR AL! VOTE FOR AL! FREE NICE HATS FOR ALL! VOTE FOR AL! VOTE FOR AL!

Now, I just need to get those rosettes printed.

Cat Shows

It came as quite a surprise to me, I can tell you, when, at the age of 28 (in cat years), I discovered that cat shows existed. Human servants escort their cats to some amphitheatre where they show us gorgeous creatures off and we perhaps win prizes if we are judged extremely gorgeous.

I'm extremely gorgeous! Why hadn't I been 'shown' before?! I assumed that my human servants were blind and/or stupid and sulked for 18 days (pausing only to deign to eat the food offered – and they should think themselves lucky. I was prepared to go on hunger strike, really I was).

Turned out there's something called pedigree, which I'd always thought involved smoked haddock, but no. It's all about breeding. Seems there are some cats who consider themselves better than others! Which is a bit like imagining that you're king – of the kings. Pfffft.

I put up with the situation for far too long, simmering quietly in my indignation, until last year when I decided to stage a cat show of my own – knowing (secretly) that I, alone, could win.

'AL'S FAMOUS CAT SHOW!'

(Being the inaugural one, it wasn't really famous, of course, but who cares – everyone talks things up these days, it's all the rage.)

THERE WERE FIVE EVENTS:

LYING AROUND A BIT

Playing comatose. Points deducted for twitches of the tail, eyelid flickers, that kind of thing.

LYING AROUND A BIT MORE

The timed round. One of the more elderly judges died of old age during this event, such was my dedication to doing naff all.

Honestly, I could write a book on this sort of thing – and indeed have done!

GETTING COMFORTABLE

Here, it got trickier. I wanted to test myself. This round was all about artistry. The padding of the paws, the swivel, the lowering, the nestle. Points awarded for grace, style, arrogance and blatant showboating.

CHANGING SPOTS ON THE SOFA

Moving into truly advanced cat skills now. How to raise oneself from slumber, move a pace or two – no more! – in a suitably feline manner, then resume one's repose, while looking like a shadow gliding on oil. This sorted the men from the boys! (And the ladies from the girls... Or it would have done, had I invited any. Imagine losing to a girl! I'd never hear the end of it!)

ACTUALLY DOING SOMETHING, LIKE CATCHING A MOUSE MAYBE? HELLO?!

A trick round, of course. Any contestant actually hunting for mice was immediately disqualified, and scorn poured upon them until they left town. I'll tell you how I negotiated this one: I got one of my human servants to ring Rentokil.

Of course, you're all now on tenterhooks! I hear you say: 'Who won, Al? Who won?'

Well, I did, of course. I told you I'd made sure I alone could win.

How?

I was the only contestant! I'm not giving that sad-sack mothball of a moggy next door the opportunity to upstage me!

Coin Tricks

These are great fun and a perfect way to amaze your friends and family. And they're so simple. They are also a great way of making yourself more popular. All you need is:

a coin!

So, here we go. This is called the French Drop. Hold the coin by the edge... Ah, I've just spotted the flaw in this plan.

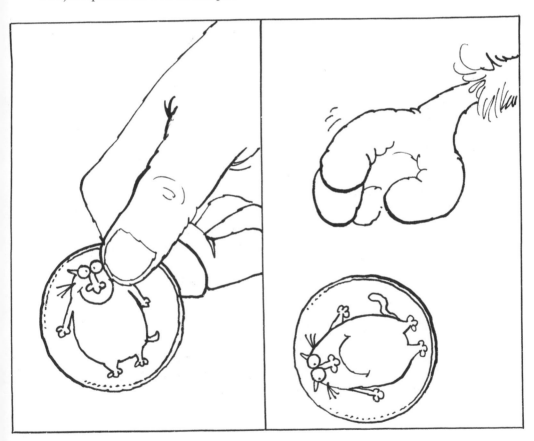

Opposable thumbs make this trick a good deal easier

Cat Proverbs (And What They Really Mean)

'Books and cats and fair-haired little girls make the best
furnishing for a room'
If all the chairs are taken, sit on a cat.

'A cat may look at a king'
If there's a king around, don't expect a cat to look the other way.

'Curiosity killed the cat, Satisfaction
brought it back!'
The Rolling Stones are better than Curiosity Killed the Cat.

'You will always be lucky if you know how to make
friends with strange cats'
Fortune favours the brave.

'I gave an order to a cat, and the cat gave it to its tail'
Please be seated, the cat's tail will bring your burger and fries
to your table.

'In a cat's eye, all things belong to cats'
Blindfold your cat or lose everything.

'The cat loves fish, but she's loath to wet her feet'
Someone give that cat a fishing rod.

'An old cat will not learn how to dance'
Only young cats can can-can.

'After dark all cats are leopards'
No, I can't see a darned thing either. Is that a cat or a leopard?

'Keep an eye on the cat and another on the frying pan'
Cats covet frying pans.

'Beware of people who dislike cats'
Anyone who dislikes cats may be carrying a gun.

'The cat was created when the lion sneezed'
Cats are made of lion snot.

'A cat is a tiger that is fed by hand'
Cats are wimps.

'A cat is a lion in a jungle of small bushes'
No, really – cats are wimps.

'Cats, flies and women are ever at their toilets'
Look, I think we'll leave it there.

Things for Cats to Build

4. House

YOU WiLL NEED:

Bricks	Nails and screws
Mortar	Power tools
Sand	Plaster
Scaffolding	Tiles
Wood	
Wire	... Hoi! Wake up!
Paint	
Fuse boxes	Electrical stuff
Copper pipe	Wallpaper
Bathroom furniture	Carpets
More wood	Fixtures and fittings
	Fittings and fixtures.

INSTRUCTIONS:

Wake up! Right. First you need to lay your foundations, otherwise your house will fall into the ground. That's right – we don't want that. I hope for your sake that wasn't sarcasm, mister.

So. Mix up your concrete using mortar, sand and water, mark out your foundations and pour in the concrete. Allow to set.

What do you think comes next? Hello? Have you painted eyes on your eyelids?! You bloody have! Rub that off this minute!

It pays to look the part for a hard day's work

Now concentrate!

What do you think comes next?

No, not a tea break.

No? All right, I'll tell you. It's the walls. We need to build the walls, using bricks and mortar. Otherwise the wind and burglars will get in. That's right, we wouldn't want that either.

I'm warning you.

OK, so once our walls are up, what would we need to build next? Here's a clue: the rain.

Look, you shouldn't need to pin your eyelids open using matchsticks! You've only been here three minutes!

Take those out!

Yes, both of them.

Right, as I was saying…

Wake up!

You were asleep – I heard you snoring!

Where were we? Oh yes: rain. What do you think we should build to keep the rain out?

A what?

A bipolar antigravity ultraviolet capacitance engine?

Well, no. The answer I'm looking for is: a roof.

Yes, oh, one of those!

A roof. So that's a wooden frame, lined with roofing felt and tiles laid on top.

[Sigh] Yes, you can go to the toilet. But be quick.

[Drums claws. Looks at watch. Drums claws some more. Looks at watch again. Goes out to check toilet. Finds it empty.]

Right, that's enough for today, then. Good work, everyone. Same time tomorrow…

HARD AT WORK ON A HOUSE

How to Avoid Being Neutered

I'm afraid I can't help female cats – all that internal organ stuff is far too complicated. (I don't know everything, you know.) However, I can help males*.

YOU WILL NEED:

- Two pickled walnuts
- A mini hot dog
- Cocktail stick.

ASSEMBLE THE ITEMS AS ABOVE:

Simply attach to the old undercarriage with string and waltz into the vets with your tail held high!

* DISCLAIMER: ADMITTEDLY THIS MIGHT NOT FOOL THEM. I KNOW WHEN I TRIED IT, THE VET SCOFFED THE NUTS AND THE SAUSAGE AND I WOKE UP MIAOWING IN A VERY HIGH VOICE.

Cats in Fashion

Cats are so hip that humans even name their fashions after us. Catsuits, kitten heels, pussy bows… We don't need any of that stuff because fashion comes naturally to us.

The same could not be said of dogs, who generally look like this:

… until, that is, their owner gets to them, then this happens:

That's why they call them dogs!!

How To... Become a Ship's Cat

asy! Find a ship and present yourself to its captain, proffering your CV. Obviously, previous experience will work in your favour; in the likely event that you have none (having previously lain around on your fat bottom all day, while being fed kippers and caviar), I recommend you insert the following in the Interests section of your CV (see below):

INTERESTS

🐾 Catching mice and rats

🐾 Being lucky

🐾 Being easier on the eye than a bloke with one or no legs.

The job's as good as yours, my fine feline friend!

Some Famous Ship's Cats

 number of ship's cats are revered in the history books, for their daring, their brains and their downright sexiness. Undeniably, the cat was the crucial component in any ship. Here is but a small selection of my favourites:

Lardy

Lardy was a big ginger tom who served aboard Vice-Admiral Horatio Nelson's flagship, HMS *Victory*, during the wars with Spain and France. While Nelson and his men sent cannonballs into the enemy bows, Lardy was below decks scoffing all their supplies while not catching mice and rats. How did he get away with such insubordination? Because he was Nelson's favourite.

The eye-patched Vice-Admiral would often hoist him on to his shoulder – with the help of ten burly men, since Lardy was a fat sod – and get the big ginger tom to be his other eye and ears, scanning the horizon for enemy vessels.

Of course, as history records, tragedy struck at the Battle of Trafalgar. Vice-Admiral Nelson lay dying, downed by a French bullet, but he managed to say a few last words. However, he did not say, as the books record, 'Kiss me, Hardy' (referring to the redoubtable Captain Hardy) – no, what he actually said was, 'Kiss me, Lardy' (referring to his favourite crew member).

Unfortunately, Lardy was downstairs at the time, scoffing the last of the biscuits.

Missy

Katharine Hepburn's cat on the *African Queen*, Missy, didn't much take to Humphrey Bogart – all that a-cussin' an' a-reekin' of oil, booze and cigarettes. So she hid away below decks (which is why you might never have noticed her). However, Missy was to play a significant role in Hepburn and Bogart's fate.

Everyone seems to believe that the two humans had rigged up the makeshift torpedo tubes on the *African Queen*, which detonated when the German gunboat, *Empress Louisa*, struck it. Not so. (Funnily enough.)

Those torpedo tubes would never have worked! What actually happened was this: Missy had not been wasting her time below decks. No, sir, she'd been working her way studiously through Bogart's shipping manuals, paying particular attention to *Manual 27: German Gunboat Sabotage For Cats*.

Don't ask me how, because Missy was lost in her own explosion – sniffle – but that plucky lady-cat saved the lives of both Hepburn and Bogart – and received not a jot of thanks or recognition for it. (And you wonder why we cats sometimes come across as uppity?)

Leopold

Leopold, a small black cat, lived on board the infamous HMS *Bounty*, captained by William Bligh. The superstitious Bligh liked the cat and considered him lucky. On 28 April 1789, during a day of particularly nice weather off the coast of Tahiti, the captain turned to the cat and declared, 'Today is indeed a lucky day, thanks to you, Leopold!'

Shortly afterwards the crew revolted and Fletcher Christian threatened Bligh with a sturdy bayonet, saying, 'I am in hell! I am in hell!'

Bligh never trusted Leopold again and the cat was forced to live with Fletcher Christian on Pitcairn Island, where his only friend was a mosquito named Morpeth.

Dave

Dave was a mangy old black cat who lived aboard Blackbeard's pirate ship. Blackbeard, being a pirate, couldn't be trusted. One day, in a fit of anger, he tossed Dave overboard, then immediately wished he hadn't. His luck rapidly disappeared over the horizon, and the festering old reprobate died of musket ball and broadsword wounds once the British Navy had dealt with him. When last seen, Blackbeard's headless corpse was swimming in ever-decreasing circles around his sinking ship, as Dave floated gently by on some driftwood, heading for the Bahamas. The moral of this story? Never toss a mangy old black cat overboard. A mangy old black cat is for life, not just for Christmas.

The Secret World of Cats

My human servants are often asking me: 'Where do you go to at night, when you leave the house? What is the secret world of cats?' They're mystified, enraptured, jealous.

Well, since I'm writing this book, I shall reveal our amazing secret. Drum roll and trumpet fanfare, please...

I sit in the garden.

Games Cats Can Play

3. Finding a Box and Sitting In It

his is one of my favourites, since it combines two of my best-loved pastimes: namely, Finding Boxes and Sitting Down. That may sound simplistic, but it's the simple things that make life such a pleasure. I'm also a huge fan of:

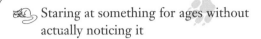

> - Staring at something for ages without actually noticing it
>
> - Flicking my tail distractedly
>
> - Lying anywhere that forces my human servants to step around me
>
> - Lying upside down with my legs in strange positions
>
> - Lying around in general.

Back to the Finding a Box and Sitting In It game. Straightforward as it seems, there are a few caveats to bear in mind:

> - Don't confuse boxes with bins. Especially just before Dustbin Day.
>
> - Don't sit in a box just before Christmas, or you might have to wait a while to get out, by which time you will definitely be needing a wee.
>
> - Never sit in a box if your human servants are in the removals business.

Once certain that your box is safe, climb in, sit down. It's hardly rocket science; anyone wishing it was is referred to *Feline Life Manual no. 162: Hoi! Cat! Here's Why Rocket Science Isn't For You!*

Famous Cats in History

5. The Pink Panther

Let's get this straight right now. There are black panthers. There are even white panthers. But there are no pink panthers. Don't exist. They're merely a figment of someone's fertile imagination.

You want proof? Look no further than the lyrics to the theme song, which try to brainwash you into a series of false beliefs. I shall deconstruct them here for you:

> **Think of all the animals you've ever heard about,**
> **like rhinoceroses and tigers, cats and mink,**
> *(Yes, I have heard of those.)*
>
> **There are lots of funny animals in all this world,**
> *(Indeed there are. Consider the duck-billed platypus.)*
> **but have you ever seen a panther that is pink?**
> *(No.)*
>
> **Think!**
> *(I did!)*
>
> **A panther that is positively pink,**
> *(Still no.)*
>
> **Well here he is, the pink panther,**
> *(No he isn't.)*
> **the rinky-dink panther,**
> *(That's just stupid.)*
> **isn't he a panther ever so pink?**
> *(NO.)*

He really is a groovy cat,
and what a gentleman, a scholar, what an acrobat!
(You're just compounding the lie now.)

He's in the pink, the pink panther,
the rinky-dink …
(I'm going now. Bye-bye!)

The Cat o' Nine Tails

There are many who say the infamous cat o' nine tails was a whip. A fearsome, dreaded whip bearing nine tails – hence that bit of the name – which could flail the hide off a man's back, soon as look at him. (Or actually when you whipped him with it, but 'soon as look at him' sounded better.) But how did a whip come to be named after a cat?, you ask. (Well, ask it now then.) It went like this…

There was once a cat named Grimble who was terribly vain and who was extremely fond of his tail. Grimble was convinced that he had the loveliest, sleekest tail in all the land. He was very proud of his tail. Too proud of his tail, some would say.

One day, Grimble was playing around with a shiny tin of cat food, pawing at it, when he rubbed a sensitive point on the tin – and a genie appeared! A rare occurrence, I know, but it happened. Trust me.

'Grimble, o Grimble, I am the Genie of the Tin,' said the Genie, 'and I shall grant you nine wishes!' (I know genies normally give out three, but it's not an exact science. This one gave out nine.)

Wow, thought Grimble. What could I possibly ask for? And then he realized, if his one tail looked that amazing, how amazing would two be?!

'I wish I had another tail,' said Grimble.

'Your wish is my command!' said the Genie.

And 'ping!', Grimble had a second tail, which he admired very much.

Now, Grimble wasn't the most imaginative of cats – and he was terribly vain – so when it came to his second wish, all he could think of was another tail. So he asked the Genie for a further tail.

'Your wish is my command!' said the Genie.

And 'ping!', Grimble had a third tail, which he admired very much.

On his third wish, Grimble did briefly consider a nice waistcoat or a colourful cravat, but thought better of it and plumped for yet another tail. Now he had four tails! And he admired them all very much.

'Look at my gorgeous tails,' Grimble would say to passing cats, and even when they replied, 'Looks flipping stupid to me,' he wasn't to be swayed. Grimble was just too vain to listen to common sense.

I'll fast-forward now, or this might turn into a shaggy-cat story…

So Grimble was on his ninth and final wish. He had nine tails now – that's eight new ones, plus his original tail, in case you're confused – and even he was starting to reconsider his own logic. Lovely as all his tails were, having so many of them was getting a little bit unwieldy.

'You have one final wish remaining,' said the Genie. 'What is that wish?'

Grimble replied, 'Oh woe, great Genie, I just don't know what to wish for. I'm tired of having all these tails, admirable as they are…'

'You could always wish for them to be gone!' said the Genie, helpfully.

'Oh, clever Genie! I wish I'd thought of that!' said Grimble. 'Your wish is my command!' said the Genie. And Grimble did think of that!

'Right!' said Grimble. 'I wish all my new tails were gone!'

But nothing happened. The Genie had long since returned to his tin of cat food. 'Hoi!' cried Grimble. 'Where have you gone?'

The Genie's muffled voice came from inside the tin: 'You've had all your nine wishes, you git!'

These events had a disastrous effect on Grimble. Dismayed at the ludicrous number of tails he now possessed, he vowed never to show his face in public again, so he put a large paper bag over his head [as shown opposite]. But what was he to do with the rest of his life?

This is where the whip bit comes in. This was back in the days when punishing people severely was very popular. Burnings, tarrings, iron maidens, stocks, pillories and racks – that sort of thing. And brutal whippings! Hurrah!

A fierce naval taskmaster by the name of Higgins chanced upon Grimble, looking all sorry for himself. And Higgins, seeing the nine tails, had a bright idea. He grabbed Grimble and started whipping insubordinate seamen with him! Nine times the agony!

So Grimble ended his days passing from fleet to fleet and being swung around lustily, which became terribly wearing. However, his vanity was at last appeased because his nine tails did indeed go down in history.

Just for all the wrong reasons.

Ten Reasons Cats Are The Best

Not everyone is convinced that we cats are the most amazing creatures in the universe. Madness, I know! Here, for those doubters, is my conclusive list of incontrovertible cat facts:

1. Cats can see in the dark better than any other creature in the world, even though we don't like carrots.

2. Even though Alexander Fleming took the credit for discovering penicillin, it was actually his cat, Tiddles, who made the breakthrough. Tiddles had let some food that wasn't up to his exacting standards go mouldy. However, he was obliged to eat it later because Fleming was forever busy tinkering in his laboratory. Only when Tiddles astonishingly recovered from tonsillitis did the scientist put two and two together.

3. Edmund Hillary is credited with conquering Everest, but it was actually his cat, Mr Stiltskin, who got there first. Hillary had said to the cat, 'Look here, Mr Stiltskin, why don't you pop up top before me, and check how cold it is? I'm worried I haven't packed enough socks, you see.' So Mr Stiltskin climbed Everest – with a mild harumph, I would admit – and returned to base camp to inform Hillary that, yes, it was a touch nippy up there, but that three pairs of socks would probably do the trick. Hillary, newly confident, since his Mum had indeed packed just that number of socks, completed the climb.

4. Alexander Graham Bell's cat, Chopper, actually invented the telephone first, using two cans and a length of string.

5. First animal in space? Not Laika the dog, as is often said, but a Russian cat by the name of Tsarina. (Admittedly, being tied to a big firework wasn't what she had had in mind. However, making history is not without its sacrifices.)

6. Michelangelo's cat, Versace, painted the Sistine Chapel ceiling while Signor Angelo was hanging out in a local bar.

7. And Leonardo da Vinci was actually a cat in disguise, hence the beard and funny hat.

8. Cats were on the moon long before man. Listen again to Neil Armstrong's little speech, as he sets foot on the surface: 'That's one small step for a man, one giant... Heck! What are all these felines doing up here?! Buzz! Buzz! We got any cream substitute in the lunar module?'

9. Cats could bake the most delicious cake in the world. (If they wanted to.)

10. Cats can stretch out further for their size than any other animal. This ability is ingrained in our DNA, in order that just one of us can cover every seat of even the world's longest sofa.

Why Do Humans Keep Tripping Over Us?

At a conservative estimate, my human servants trip over me on average 17.5 times a day, which is roughly 6,387.5 times a year. This is a painful statistic whichever way you look at it. It doesn't matter where I lie down:

- In the middle of the hallway…

- Halfway up the stairs…

- Camouflaged against the lounge carpet, right in the doorway…

… they always trip over me! Are they completely blind?!

Being Owned by a Dotty Old Lady

You know the type: retired, never been married, has a larder full of food way past its sell-by date, wears a bonnet which matches her shopping trolley, keeps 100 cats around the house, doesn't have a cat-flap. This sort of thing. But how do you escape from this situation if you are of the feline persuasion? Stuck indoors all day, every day, with 99 other cats for company. It's not just that the litter tray's overflowing, the old dear herself is incontinent.

Every day the council people bang on the door. 'Ms So-and-So, please let us in, we've had reports that you're keeping too many cats!' And she will not let them in.

You're thinking, 'Actually, a little fresh air wouldn't go amiss, and it is a tad crowded in here.' And still she sits there, the stubborn old moo.

HERE'S WHAT TO DO:

What's the one thing guaranteed to get an old lady moving? That's right – anything at all on Special Offer.

So just knock up a few fake 'SALE' leaflets – anything will do: furniture, beans, garden gnomes, shrunken heads; the less she actually needs it, the better. Put them on the doormat and rattle the letterbox. She won't be able to resist a look – and when she reads those leaflets, she'll be out of there quicker than you can say 'rumpled tights'.

Be ready. As the door opens – LEG IT!

Cat's Eyes

Could you ever imagine a crueller article? The person who invented the road-safety device, whose name I cannot bring myself to utter – actually I don't know it, so let's refer to him as 'John' – must have seen the light reflected in a cat's eyes, and thought to himself, 'They'd be handy, plonked at equal intervals along the middle of a road at night!'

So he gathers up a series of stray cats, puts them in boxes and lines them up down the middle of a road.

Imagine the terror those poor cats must have experienced, having cars shooting by on either side in the middle of the night!

(YES, I'M NOT QUITE SURE YOU'VE GOT A FIRM GRIP ON THIS ONE – ED.)

John should be ashamed of himself! If I got my claws on John…

(THEY WEREN'T REAL CATS' EYES – ED.)

No?

(NO. JOHN – OR PERCY SHAW AS HE WAS BETTER KNOWN – MERELY USED REAL CAT'S EYES AS THE INSPIRATION FOR THE MANUFACTURE OF A SIMILAR TYPE OF REFLECTIVE DEVICE – ED.)

Was that the gong for tea? I really must be going.

Famous Cat Lovers 9
Edward Lear designed a coat of arms for his toast-eating tabby, Foss, and wrote a poem in which a cat mysteriously marries a bird of prey. He also had a house designed like his previous dwelling so Foss wouldn't be upset when they moved. Did he really imagine Foss wouldn't notice?! So the cat moved next door, where her new owner fed her proper food not crummy old toast. Talk about cheapskates.

If Cats Ruled the World...

Imagine if cats ruled the world, what a gorgeous, safe(ish) place it would be! You'd have mice on tap and dogs wouldn't get a look-in. Here are some laws I would pass:

1. THE OBSEQUIOUSNESS LAW

Human servants are required to be obsequious to cats at all times. A simple 'Hello, kitty!' will not do. Human servants should think along the lines of: 'My, you're looking hot today' or 'Your loveliness makes me feel like a turnip in comparison.'

2. THE FOOD FOR ALL LAW

We cats shouldn't have to wait for our specific human servants to provide us with food. (I once had to wait 24 hours for the next square meal, when my human servants were too wrapped up in themselves. [What's a 'family funeral' anyway?]) So all human servants should place five bowls of decent food – none of your tinned rubbish, more fresh salmon and caviar, that sort of thing – outside their front doors at 7am each morning, so passing cats may feast. Any human servant not complying with this is to be used as a scratching pole by 17 sturdy cats. (No, I don't consider that too harsh.)

3. THE FREEDOM OF MOVEMENT LAW

There shall be no more 'house cats' – a slur upon our very name. Any human servants not providing a cat-flap within 24 hours of being served notice shall have their dwelling demolished, which should leave a hole quite large enough for their cat to enter and exit freely.

4. THE YOU-CATCH-IT-IF-YOU'RE-SO-FLIPPING-WORRIED-ABOUT-IT LAW

While hunting and slaying mice might be instilled in our DNA, I do sometimes find it demeaning. It's as if the human servants think it's all we're good for! So human servants must now catch their own mice, leaving us more time to grab some well-earned shut-eye.

5. THE SOFA LAW

All sofas and armchairs are to be handed over to we cats forthwith. Any human servant attempting to actually get too comfortable is to be tied to a bed of nails and exported to Latvia.

6. THE WAR LAW

We cats do like fighting. Just can't help ourselves. However, we should really justify any such hostilities, so any other cat deemed to be in ownership of a White Meal Dish (WMD) shall be forthwith declared fair game.

7. THE CATS-FIRST LAW

How often I have had to wait for a human servant to finish what they are doing before attending to me. I'll give you an example: one morning I was waiting patiently (well, not that patiently; actually I was moaning like a ghost that's stubbed its toe) for my litter tray to be cleaned out – and my human servant's lying on the floor, if you please, having some sort of medical emergency! 'Call an ambulance!' he cries. No problem at all, I think – *once you've sifted out all those claggy lumps of grit.* This situation has to stop. Cats must be given precedence at all times of the day and night.

8. THE CARPET LAW

Frankly, any surface that isn't carpeted can be a little chilly on the paws. So I propose carpeting the entire world. (No, I don't think that's excessive. Yes, and the lakes and oceans. Well, find some floating carpet then! Sheesh, you really can't get the staff these days.)

Right, everyone in favour, say, 'Aye!'
Erm, hello? I can't hear you…

How to Repay Hospitality

While we can quite capably look after ourselves, there should come a time – not a terribly long time, admittedly – in every cat's life when they think to themselves, 'You know, my human servants are very slightly good to me on deeply rare occasions.' (I know, we're all heart.) 'I really should repay them somehow… But how?'

I've considered this quandary myself before, and ended up with this list:

CHOCOLATES

FLOWERS

CASH

BOOK TOKENS

CHAMPAGNE

OR WINE

PHOTOGRAPH ALBUM

GADGET

UNDERWEAR

CDs

BOOKS

JEWELLERY

CLOCK OR WATCH

GIFT VOUCHERS

But I looked down that list and I thought, 'Nah'. If I wouldn't want any of that stuff, why would they? None of that's any use – it's just clutter. Then I had a brainwave…

What every human servant really, really wants is a small dead animal! Perhaps lobbed on to their floor awaiting their arrival. Ideally, you will have mauled it about a bit first.

And dragged it in from outside in the middle of the night, so there's a chance they might step on it when going for a wee.

Oh yes, that's right there at the top of their Christmas list.

Black Cats - Are They Lucky?

It is a common superstition among our human servants that if a black cat crosses their path then good luck will come their way. But no one said anything about night-time.

I have a friend named Merlin who is a black cat. He crossed his human servant's path on the landing one night, tripping him over. The human fell down two flights of stairs, breaking his collarbone, six vertebrae, his jaw and his little finger. He lay there unconscious for three days, wet himself and was eventually discovered by a neighbour who heard his weak cries.

While he was recovering in hospital he lost his job and picked up MRSA, his wife went off with another man, who turned out to be the world's most successful and merciless divorce lawyer who could normally only be afforded by Hollywood stars, members of rock groups and people on the boards of oil companies, his house was repossessed and his parents phoned to say that actually he'd been adopted, that nobody knew his real parents, that they'd never liked him anyway and would he please sod off.

Lucky? I think not.

Cuteness and How to Deal With It

Humans do so love a cute ickle kitten, or preferably three cute ickle kittens, cuddwing up to each uvver. They plaster them all over birthday cards, posters, plates... Cats on plates? What's all that about?

To which I say:

NO!

Cuteness must be stamped out. We are in this for ourselves, not for anyone else. Making a human's heart skip a beat and for them to go, 'Aw, Aren't they CUTE?!' is tantamount to prostitution.

In case you're thinking, 'Weren't *you* a cute kitten once?':

NO! NO! NO!

I wasn't. Immediately after I was born, I rolled myself in tar then a succession of unattractive litter-based objects, such as pork pie crusts, mutilated Jelly Babies, a postcard of Basingstoke, two hairclips discarded by a lady with greasy hair and nits, and some poo. (I later regretted the last item – you try getting tar and poo out of your fur.)

So, anytime you spot an ornament or 'living sculpture' featuring our cuddly kin, simply rig up the apparatus shown below*. And Do The Right Thing.

* DYNAMITE WOULD ALSO SUFFICE

Things for Cats to Build

5: Fish Ladder

 fish ladder is an ingenious device invented by humans, which helps fish to get about without having to take unhealthy shortcuts across dry land. Fish just love travelling up fish ladders, which got me thinking…

What if I built my own fish ladder? Perhaps I could get that idiot goldfish to leap up the ladder and into my waiting gob.

YOU WILL NEED:

- Lots of fish
- Some string (for binding).

INSTRUCTIONS:

1. Bind the fish together until they resemble a ladder.

2. Put your fish ladder in the goldfish bowl.

3. Wait!

4. If you think I may be missing something obvious, please keep it to yourself.

Some Things Cats Might Say
(If They Could Talk Human)

Sometimes it's a bummer not having the power of human speech. Sure, we cats have intonation and immense pester power, but our human servants still never seem to understand us. Some examples:

HUMAN: 'Here, Kitty! Come get your food!'

CAT: 'Miaow!'

WHAT WE'D ACTUALLY LIKE TO SAY: 'You call that food?! If I sicked that up, I'd be ashamed of myself! You monster!'

HUMAN: 'Why don't you come and sit over here with me?'

CAT: 'Miaow!'

WHAT WE'D ACTUALLY LIKE TO SAY: 'Sit with you?! Do you think I've had a nasal bypass operation? If I lay in your lap, my head would fall off!'

HUMAN [scratching cat]: 'Is that nice?'

CAT: 'Miaow!'

WHAT WE'D ACTUALLY LIKE TO SAY: 'No, it's not bloody nice! You're in completely the wrong place, you ham-fisted oaf! In truth, you've been scratching the same bit of my head for so long, it's starting to chafe. I can't wait until you get your vet bills! Then you'll be sorry!'

HUMAN [to human friend]: 'The cat seems to love it here!'

CAT: 'Miaow!'

WHAT WE'D ACTUALLY LIKE TO SAY: 'NO, I DON'T! This is the worst place in the world! It's Guantanamo Bay times a million! You're worse than Genghis Khan!'

And that's just the tip of the iceberg. Here are some other things cats might like to be able to say:

> ...'Yes, yes, you can go now!'
>
> ...'No!'
>
> ...'If you can't control your children, I suggest you put them in a home!'
>
> ...'I am trying to relax!'
>
> ...'Yes, it has been a hard day, actually!'
>
> ...'All right then – you terrorize the small bird!'
>
> ...'Open the door!'
>
> ...'No, I don't feel stupid, actually!'
>
> ...'How dare you!'

Some Things Cats Might Do
(If They Had Opposable Thumbs)

I t is so excruciating, not being able to open a door. Sometimes you're scratch-scratch-scratching away and you can hear them, on the other side, ignoring you deliberately. Oh, the ignominy. The scenario goes something like this:

> HUMAN ENTERS ROOM. SHUTS DOOR.
> Cat thinks, 'Wait! Wait! I'm just behind you! Don't shut... the... Door.' Sigh.
> Cat scratches at door for hours, eventually wishing was dead.
>
> HUMAN IS EATING YUMMY CHICKEN.
> Cat sits beside human, eyeing food enviously. 'Miaow!'
> HUMAN: 'I JUST GAVE YOU YOUR FOOD!'
> Cat remains there, staring, hoping against hope. 'Miaow!'
> HUMAN EATS FINAL MORSEL.
> Cat sniffs at plate. Licks glaze. Wishes was dead.
>
> HUMAN IS DANGLING STRING ABOVE CAT, PULLING IT OUT OF REACH EVERY
> TIME THE CAT LUNGES.
> Cat finally gets a single claw into the string.
> HUMAN TUGS STRING FROM CAT'S GRASP. CHUCKLES.
> Cat wishes was dead.

Right, now, let's replay those same three scenes, but this time imagining that the cat has opposable thumbs...

> HUMAN ENTERS ROOM. SHUTS DOOR.
> Cat thinks, 'Wait! Wait! I'm just behind you! Don't shut... the... Door.' Sigh.
> Cat opens door, grabs human, pushes head through door.

HUMAN IS EATING YUMMY CHICKEN.
Cat sits beside human, eyeing food enviously. 'Miaow!'
HUMAN: 'I JUST GAVE YOU YOUR FOOD!'
Cat grabs plate, tips contents into gob, breaks plate over human's head.

HUMAN IS DANGLING STRING ABOVE CAT, PULLING IT OUT OF REACH EVERY
TIME THE CAT LUNGES.
Cat sets fire to string with lighter, burns human's fingers.

So you see, if only we had opposable thumbs, life would be so much more pleasant all round.

Famous Cat Poets: An Occasional Series*

* WHEN I SAY 'OCCASIONAL', WHAT I REALLY MEAN IS THIS IS WITHOUT QUESTION THE ONLY ONE. SO MAKE THE MOST OF IT.

1. TS Eliot

T S Eliot was – he's dead now – a poet who had a fascination for cats. He wrote lots of light-hearted poems about us, which other humans found hilarious. Personally, I find him overrated. I mean, who can't write a funny poem about cats? Here's one of mine:

> **There was a cat named Sepulchre Who...**
>
> Hang on, start again. I may have made work for myself there.
>
> **The cat spotted the wolf And...**
>
> Nope.
>
> **The cat got stuck in the chimney...**
> **The cat rested on its elbow...**
> **The cat spotted a mouse...**
> **The cat put in for redundancy...**
> **The cat found some gunpowder...**
> **The cat swallowed an iron...**
> **The cat ran the marathon...**
> **The cat composed a fugue...**
> **The cat spotted the syzygy...**

Sod this for a game of soldiers. TS Eliot was a great poet. Let's forget this ever happened, OK?

Ciao!

So there you have it. The End. I bet you've learnt more reading my book than you would have done had you read every other book in the world, such as *The Big Book of Cats*, *The Bigger Book of Cats* and… (er) *The Slightly Smaller Book of Cats*? Yes, I can think of more books than that, I just choose not to list them all here.

Let me sum up all you have learned from this notable compendium in a simple list:

Always be true to yourself (which is different from being selfish. A bit.)
Lie around
Love yourself

Catch mice
Antagonize mice
Tease mice
Show them who's boss

Agitate
Rest
Elongate

Grow wise
Respect others (other cats, that is)
Eat for free
Accept all favours
Triumph!

Spot that clever acronym? Commit it to memory and you shall live long and prosper. I'm outta here.

Ciao, baby!

Al x